BIBLE STORIES
FOR THE
CHURCH YEAR

BIBLE STORIES
FOR THE
CHURCH YEAR

KRISTEN JOHNSON INGRAM

Joseph P. Russell, Consulting Editor

Pamela Ford Johnson, Illustrator

A Vineyard Book

1817

Harper & Row, Publishers, San Francisco
Cambridge, Hagerstown, New York, Philadelphia, Washington
London, Mexico City, São Paulo, Singapore, Sydney

Library of Congress Cataloging-in-Publication Data

Ingram, Kristen Johnson.
    Bible stories for the church year.

    "A Vineyard book."
    Summary: More than 125 Bible stories with a chart for correlating them with the lectionaries of various churches.
    1. Bible stories, English. 2. Lectionaries.
[1. Bible stories] I. Johnson, Pamela Ford, ill.
II. Title.
BS551.2.I55   1986   220.9′505   86-50172
ISBN 0-86683-537-7

87 88 89 90 91 RRD 10 9 8 7 6 5 4 3 2 1

Contents

Jesus and the Little Girl;   The Man Who Was Born Blind;   The Sower;
The Wheat and the Weeds;   Jesus Sends Seventy-Two People to Teach;
The Good Samaritan;   Mary and Martha;   The Good Shepherd;   The
Lord's Prayer; Jesus Walks on Water;   Invited to a Feast;   The Lost Sheep;
The Prodigal Son;   Jesus Heals a Deaf Man;   Peter Is Given His Name; The
Wicked Servant;   The Workers in the Vineyard;   Jesus Heals Ten Men; Two
Sons; Invitations to a Wedding;   The Poor Woman and the Judge; Jesus
Talks about the Law of Israel;   The Pharisee and the Tax Collector;
Zacchaeus in the Sycamore Tree;   The Transfiguration of Jesus;   Jesus and
His Friend Lazarus;   The Blind Beggar;   The Widow's Penny;   Being Ready
for God; Ten Women with Their Lamps;   A Story about Money;   The Sheep
and the Goats;   A Woman Washes Jesus' Feet;   Jesus Rides into Jerusalem;
Jesus in the Temple;   The Last Supper;   Jesus Washes His Disciples' Feet;
Jesus Goes to the Cross;   The First Easter;   Thomas Sees the Risen Lord;
The Road to Emmaus;   Peter Goes Fishing;   Jesus Goes to His Father; The
Pentecost Story;   The Man at the Beautiful Gate;   The Apostles in Jail;
Philip and the Man from Ethiopia;   The Road to Damascus;   Peter Baptizes
a Roman;   Peter Escapes from Jail;   Paul and Barnabas Are Called Gods; An
Earthquake at the Jail;   Paul in Athens;   The Holy City

Preface

The majority of the Bible stories in this book are selections from the three-year lectionary, retold for children ages six to twelve. Although the stories are sometimes a paraphrase of the Bible, they are most often a retelling in words and concepts suitable for children. In writing and editing we experienced a constant tension between the desire to be true to the text and the desire to tell a story the children could understand and appreciate. The problems of retelling are very similar to the problems of translating colloquial writing from a foreign language into English.

In most cases, one or more of the appointed lessons has been retained for each Sunday. Among the lessons that have not been retained are those that seem inappropriate for children because of violent or otherwise mature subject matter, such as the slaughter of the innocents, the woman with the issue of blood, and the sacrifice of Isaac. Although some eschatological material is included, apocalyptic warnings are not. However, the largest number of lessons that did not seem suitable were those concerned primarily with sophisticated concepts.

A few stories not in the lectionary but popular with children, such as David and Goliath, Daniel in the lions' den, and the Joseph stories, have been added, as has the story of Ruth, since there are so few stories in the lectionary featuring women.

Because of the various concerns—pedagogical, biblical, theological, liturgical—that converge on this book, the stories have been very carefully reviewed and edited by a committee able to reflect all of these interests. The persons on this committee, who devoted many hours to this book and without whom *Bible Stories for the Church Year* could not have come into being, were Avery Brooke, Howard Galley, and Maggie Niles. To them the publisher owes special thanks.

Preface

Introduction

The Church has a story to tell. It is a story that shapes our understanding of life and death and our vision of life that is to come. The story is that found in the Bible, in the ongoing story of God's action in creation and in history, and in the story of each of our lives at the present moment. Our Christian consciousness is shaped by the stories that we share out of our own lives and out of the lives of those who have gone before us.

As I grew up, my understanding of myself, my family, and my world came out of the stories that my parents told or read to me. I knew that I was important to them because they remembered so well the story of my birth and repeated it to me every year at my birthday. My values as a child were influenced by the stories read and told at mealtime and at bedtime. I gained a sense of historic and ethical consciousness from the stories told about what had happened in the wider world of my parents and the stories they repeated with joy or concern from the daily newspaper. I felt family pride and continuity as I heard the stories of my ancestors.

As we grow up in the Christian family that is the Church, we are influenced by the same kind of story-sharing. The worship of the Church is story-formed. As we gather for worship on Sunday, feast day, or ordinary day, we are immersed in the salvation story. We hear the stories of our biblical ancestors the Jews and early Christians, who shared their experiences of God in the stories they told about God. We hear the stories of Jesus and the apostles, stories that define for us the nature of God and our role in God's world. These stories are told and interpreted each time Christians gather for worship and education. We respond to the biblical stories of faith by sharing glimpses of our own stories in the Prayers of the People and in the Confession. Behind names held out in prayer are our stories of those people and our relationship with them. Behind phrases of concern for nation and world lie our stories that lead to those concerns. In the moments of Confession our feelings of failure, guilt, regret, and frustration are expressed. At the altar the minister rehearses the sweep of the whole salvation story in the Great Thanksgiving to God for all that has been done for us in creation, in calling us out as a people and most of all in sending us

Jesus, the living presence of God in history. The story of the Last Supper, recited as bread is broken and wine is blessed, is living testimony that when the story of Jesus at table with his disciples is remembered, it becomes a living reality for disciples in every age, wherever they may be. The risen Christ is at table with us today as we gather.

The story is essential if we are to grow in Christ. What we hear in story is far more powerful than what we learn in doctrine. The Jews knew this generations before Jesus. They told their great stories (found in what Christians call the Old Testament) with conviction in a series of festivals scheduled to correspond to the natural cycles of planting and harvesting. The crucial stories of the Exodus from Egypt were told at the beginning of the spring harvest at the feast of Passover. The giving of the Law to the people through Moses at Mount Sinai was celebrated in the joyful celebration of Pentecost at the end of the spring harvest fifty days after Passover. The wandering of the Hebrews in the wilderness for forty years was re-experienced by each generation of faithful Jews at the fall harvest, the Feast of Tabernacles. In those great festivals the story was told, celebrated, and experienced anew by each generation of people who heard it. Thus the great stories told by our biblical ancestors became associated with certain seasons and festivals. Over the years a lectionary developed for sharing most of the portions of the Hebrew scripture. A lectionary is a list of readings indicating what passages of scripture are to be read on a given day. By the end of the year most of the Bible had been read and studied within the context of the various festivals and seasons.

The Christian Church as it evolved out of Judaism incorporated the idea of hearing the rapidly forming Christian story within the framework of the Jewish festivals. The Gospel of John, for example, is formed around the great Jewish feasts of Passover, Pentecost, and Tabernacles. Soon the Christians developed their own annual round of feasts, festivals, and fasts growing out of some of the Jewish seasonal celebrations. Thus early in Christian history we find both the Hebrew and Christian scriptures being read in a seasonal manner. Resurrection stories, of course, were heard at Easter. Birth stories of Jesus were shared at Christmas. Stories of baptism and the calling of the disciples were shared during Epiphany. Portions of the Hebrew scripture and epistles relating to the theme of the great Gospel stories were read at the appropriate times.

Today we have a lectionary shared ecumenically by Roman Catholics and Protestants, a lectionary that spans three years during which the entire New Testament is heard along with great segments of the Hebrew scripture. This lectionary has roots reaching back into Judaism as it existed generations before Jesus. While there are some denominational variations, especially in the Hebrew scripture, most of the lectionary is common to all liturgical traditions. The lectionary leads us season by season through every aspect of Christian faith and belief. If we follow that lectionary faithfully over the course of the year, we will have touched on every aspect of what it means to be alive in Christ, for that is what the ancient seasons of the Church year are designed to do through generations of practice. We don't have to worry about what to teach or which doctrines of belief are most essential for children and adults. The round of liturgical seasons, festivals, and fasts takes care of that question for us.

It makes sense, then, to pay attention to the readings assigned each week in the lectionary. If the Parable of the Prodigal Son is the appointed Gospel story for the Sunday, as it is on the Fourth Sunday of Lent in Year C, then we need to read or tell that story with children and adults during the week prior to the Fourth Sunday and to experience the story in the Christian education setting before or after the worship experience. A child hearing the parable read to them at bedtime on Monday evening and then hearing the story told, talked about, and experienced in a variety of ways in the Church school setting will be prepared to hear the parable with conviction when it is read as the Gospel during the Eucharist. Words of the sermon that might normally flow over the head of a child may now find a home in the consciousness of that child. Of course, what is true for children is also true for adults!

And that brings me to this book that you hold in your hands. There are many Bible story books published for children, but *Bible Stories for the Church Year* is different. Although the stories in this book are arranged in the order in which they are found in the Bible, the tables on pages 175-197 relate these stories to four specific lectionaries: (1) the Episcopal lectionary found in the Book of Common Prayer, (2) the Roman Catholic lectionary, (3) the Methodist lectionary, and (4) the Common Lectionary, now in provisional use in several denominations, including the Presbyterian Church, the United Church of Christ, and the Anglican Church of Canada. The tables will help you quickly find the story that fits with a lectionary selection that will be heard in the context of the liturgy on a given Sunday.

These stories are paraphrased to a child's understanding. This is a book made for the giving. Encourage the child to read the appointed story during the week. Read it out loud with your child. Invite the child to take the book to the liturgy and look up the story during the quiet time before the liturgy begins. The illustrations can serve as a window into the child's own prayer and meditation as the child looks at the book from time to time during the liturgy. Church school teachers will find this book a valuable resource to use as a part of their lesson plan each week.

Not every week in our three-year lectionary has an obvious story that a child can appreciate. Quite often neither the Hebrew scripture selection nor the Gospel nor the epistle text will include a story that can easily be shared with children. These are the Sundays that can be a problem for the teacher or parent wanting a story to share with children that relates to the theme of the readings. With this in mind the writer and editors have searched for appropriate stories that would illustrate the concepts of the assigned lectionary texts.

For example, on the Fourth Sunday after the Epiphany in Year C, the Gospel selection is the story about Jesus almost being killed by the people of his hometown when he told them that foreigners were more apt to acknowledge the power of God than God's own people. "And he said, 'Truly, I say to you, no prophet is acceptable in his own country'" (Luke 4:24). Jesus gave two examples of foreigners who were touched by God's power. One of them was Naaman the Syrian, who was cured of his leprosy by the prophet Elisha. Thus the story chosen from *Bible Stories for the Church Year* is "Naaman the Leper." By reading this story, the parent, child, or teacher has the benefit of hearing in detail one of the examples Jesus used to chastise his own people who could not believe in God's power with the conviction of a foreigner.

Looking at the Fifth Sunday in Lent for Year C, we find that the appointed readings include the Parable of the Tenants. The first selection is a beautiful reading from Isaiah in which the prophet compares what God is going to do in the future for the salvation of the people with what God did in the past at the time of the Exodus. The suggested readings from *Bible Stories for the Church Year* are "The Plagues and Passover" and "Crossing the Red Sea." Again the child is given the benefit of hearing the source of references made in the appointed lectionary texts.

In Year B, for the Sunday closest to August 17 the Hebrew scripture reading is from the Book of Proverbs and the Gospel selection is a part of John's poetic discourse on the narrative of Jesus feeding the five thousand. The story suggested for this week is *"The Last Supper."* Where the Gospel selection from the lectionary, from John 6, provides a theological treatment of the Eucharist, we suggest that children hear the actual story of the Last Supper.

Here then is a Bible story book for children that is designed with the ecumenical lectionary of the Church in mind. It is a resource for church school teachers, providing them with appropriate Bible stories for every week in the Church year and giving them a natural focal point for the weekly session with children. This is a resource for parents who are anxious to prepare their children for their weekly participation in the parish worship experience and who want to supplement the teaching children will receive in the church school setting. The book is a natural "take home" supplement for the Church school lesson that parents and children can share each week together. Finally, of course, this is a resource for the children who can begin to feel more at home as part of the Christian community as they take the book with them to the liturgy on a Sunday and as they read the stories during the week at home. Though the calendar of lessons makes finding the appropriate lectionary stories a simple task, the book itself is in biblical order so that as the child finds the story each week he or she is also getting a feel for the organization of the Bible.

This book expresses for the child the biblical story as it has been handed on to us by that cloud of witnesses who have told the story of their encounter with God in creation, in historic events, in the power of prophet's words, and most of all through the living experience of God revealed in Jesus the Christ. May this book of Bible stories keyed to the church's reading of scripture in worship help a new generation of Christians become aware of how God touches them in their lives, and may it encourage them to tell their stories of those encounters with the conviction of their biblical ancestors.

Joseph P. Russell
Consulting Editor

HEBREW SCRIPTURE

God Makes the Universe

Genesis 1:1–2:3

In the beginning, when God made the earth, it did not have any shape. Then God's Spirit moved over the dark waters.

God said, "Let there be light," and light came. God saw that the light was good. God called the light day and called the darkness night. The first evening and the first morning were the first day.

Then God made a separation between the earth and the sky. God called the sky heaven. That evening and that morning were the second day.

The earth was covered with water. God said, "Let dry land appear." So the water washed onto some parts of the planet, and the land came up in between. God called the water seas, or oceans. Then God said, "Let things grow on the land. Let there be plants with seeds, and fruit trees." Plants and trees grew out of the land. God saw that the land and the growing things were good. That evening and that morning were the third day.

Then God said, "Let there be a sun and moon to separate night and day." So the sun and moon were made, the sun for the daytime and the moon for nighttime. God made the stars, too. God saw that the sun and moon and stars were good. That evening and that morning were the fourth day.

After making the land and sea, God said, "Let all kinds of living things come from the oceans, and let birds fly across the sky."

So God made great sea monsters and all the other kinds of fish and animals that live in the water. God made many kinds of birds to fly in the sky.

God saw that these were good, so God said to the sea animals and birds and fish, "Grow and have many children, so that the oceans will be full of life and there will be many, many birds." That evening and that morning were the fifth day.

Then God said, "Let animals live on the land, too." So God made all kinds of animals to live on the land. God saw that they were good.

When the animals and fishes and birds were made, God said, "I will make people. I will make them in my image. Their job will be to take care of the fishes and the animals and the birds."

So God made men and women and said, "Grow, and have children to live all over the earth. You are in charge of the animals in the sea and on the land and in the sky."

God told the people, "You may have any plant with seeds in it or any fruit from the tree for food. And I have given the animals and birds green plants to eat."

God saw everything that had been made, and God knew that it was very good. And that evening and morning were the sixth day.

That is how the heavens and the earth and all the creatures and people that live in them were made. And on the seventh day God rested because the work was done. He made a seventh day for rest and blessed it and made it holy.

God Makes the First Man and Woman

Genesis 2:7–23

When God first decided to make people, God took some dust from the ground and made a man from it. He breathed into the man's nose the breath of life, and that man became alive.

God made a beautiful garden called Eden and all kinds of good trees to grow there. One of the trees was the tree of life. Another tree was called the tree of knowing good and bad.

God put the first man in the garden of Eden to take care of it. "You may eat any of the fruits or vegetables in this garden except for the fruit from the tree of knowing good and bad," God told the man. "If you eat any of that fruit, you will not live forever."

Then God said, "It is not good for the man to live all alone." So God showed the man all the animals, and the man gave these animals names. But there was no animal that could be the right kind of partner for the man.

Then God made the man fall asleep. While he was asleep, God took one of the man's ribs from his chest.

God took the rib and made it into a woman. When the man woke up, God showed him the woman.

"At last!" said the man. "Here is someone like me. She is made from my own muscles and bones."

The Garden of Eden

Genesis 3

Now of all the animals that God put into the garden of Eden, the snake was the cleverest. This snake said to the first woman, "Did God tell you not to eat any of the things that grow on the trees in this garden?"

"We may eat all the fruit we want," she told the snake. "But we may not eat any fruit from the tree of knowing good and bad. If we eat that fruit, we will die."

The snake said, "You won't die! But if you eat that fruit, you will be like God, and you will know what is good and what is bad."

The woman listened to the snake. She saw that the fruit on the tree of knowing good and bad looked delicious. She took some and ate it.

Then she gave some to the man, who was with her, and he ate some, too. Suddenly they understood what was good and what was bad. They were ashamed and hid in the garden.

When God found out what they had done, God was angry. "You ate some of the fruit that I told you not to eat," God said to the man and the woman. "Now you will have to work hard for your food. You will have to plant seeds instead of picking fruit off the trees in Eden."

Then God made Adam and Eve leave the garden of Eden forever and put an angel with a sword made from fire in front of the garden to guard it.

Noah and the Rainbow Covenant
Genesis 6:5–9:17

After Adam and Eve left the garden, people seemed to act more and more wickedly. God was angry at these people because they did not care about being good.

"The whole world is full of badness. People are fighting and hurting each other, "God said. "They are ruining the beautiful world I gave them."

So God decided to send a flood of water that would cover houses, trees, mountains, animals, and people. But God saw that there was one good family in the world. The people in this family were Noah, his wife, and their children.

God spoke to Noah. "I want you to build a big boat, called an ark."

God told Noah how to make this ark. God said, "Soon I will send a flood that will cover houses, trees, mountains, animals, and people. But I will make a promise to you. If you will build an ark and put animals and food for the animals on the ark, I will make sure that you and your family are safe from the flood."

This kind of a promise between God and people is called a covenant.

Noah did just what God asked him to. He made the ark of strong wood. He brought pairs of all kinds of animals and birds into the ark. Then he and his family got into the ark and shut the doors tightly so no water could get in.

God made rain fall for forty days and nights. All the ponds and springs and lakes and rivers ran over. All the world that Noah and his wife and their family knew was covered with water. Only the people and animals in the ark were safe.

The rain stopped, but the water stayed for half a year. Then the ark stopped floating and sat still on a mountain in Ararat.

One day Noah opened a window. He sent out a raven, but it could not find any land and kept flying. He waited. He sent out a dove, but it could not find any land, so he put out his hand and took the dove inside. He waited another week and sent the dove out again. This time it came back with a small branch of an olive tree in its beak. Then Noah knew that the land was drying out. The third time he sent the dove out, it did not come back.

Noah opened up the big doors of the ark. He looked outside. He saw dry land. Then God said to Noah, "Now you may take your family and leave the ark. Let all the animals inside go free."

Noah and his wife and their family left the ark. They turned the animals loose.

Then Noah built an altar to thank God. God was pleased and blessed Noah and his wife and their family and made a covenant with them: "Never again shall all the people and animals and plants be covered with water."

And God made a rainbow in the clouds as a sign of this promise.

The Tower of Babel

Genesis 11:1–9

Many people were born after Noah and his wife and their family left the ark. In those days all people spoke the same language.

As families grew larger, they moved into new lands. They found a valley in the east and called it the plain of Shinar. They learned to make bricks out of the clay in that valley and to bake them so that they were strong. Instead of making stone houses, as they always had before, they made houses out of bricks now.

They thought about the strong bricks they had learned to make, and they decided to build a great city with a tall tower.

"The top of our tower will be clear to the sky," they said proudly. "All people on earth will see it and know who we are. We will be famous all over the world."

God looked at the city and the tower that the people were building to reach the sky.

"They think they can do everything," God said. "They all speak the same language and understand each other. When they get together and make plans, nothing will be impossible for them."

So God sent different languages to these people. They could not understand each other, and they had to stop building the city and the tower, because they could not plan together.

After that, the people who lived near the unfinished tower called it Babel. This word meant "confusion," or "mixed up." People called the tower by that name because God mixed up the language of all the people on earth. Then God scattered the people and sent them to start new countries.

God Calls Abram
Genesis 11:28–12:9

Long ago there was a man named Abram. He and his wife, Sarai, lived in a place called Ur and then moved to a place called Haran. They had no children.

One day God called to Abram. "Abram, I want you to take Sarai and go to a new land that I will show you," God said. "I will bless you and make your children into a great nation."

Abram and Sarai did what God told them and moved to the new land, even though they were not young any more. Abram invited his brother's son Lot to go with them. They took their tents and furniture and clothes, and loaded them on animals. They collected all their sheep and goats and hired men and women to help take care of them. Then they began to walk many miles to Canaan, the new country God would show them.

When they got into Canaan, Abram and Sarai and their family and helpers went on to Shechem, to the sacred tree of Moreh. There were people already living nearby.

God came to Abram and said, "Some day I will give this land to you and your children and grandchildren and great-grandchildren." So Abram made an altar there and prayed to God. Then they all started walking toward the desert of Canaan, called the Negev.

God's Covenant with Abram
Genesis 12–15

Abram and Sarai and Abram's nephew Lot went to the Negev part of Canaan and lived there until there was not enough food for their animals. Then they moved to Egypt for a while and finally went back to Canaan.

Lot went to live near the city of Sodom, and Abram and Sarai went to live in their tents by the big trees of Mamre at Hebron in Canaan. God promised Abram and Sarai and their children all the land they could see.

One night God said to Abram, "Do not be afraid of anything, Abram. Your reward for obeying me will be great."

"What good will that do?" Abram asked. "I have no children. All the land you give me will not even belong to my own family."

"Come outside your tent," God said. Abram walked outside and looked at the sky.

"Count the stars, if you can," God told him. "The number of the stars is how many children and grandchildren and great-grandchildren you will have."

Abram believed God and trusted God, even though he was old. Because Abram trusted God, God was pleased with him. The next time God spoke to Abram, God said, "I am God, who brought your family from Ur to give you this land to own."

But Abram said, "How can I be sure I will own this land?"

God said, "Kill some animals and cut each of them into two pieces and put the pieces side by side." Abram put the meat out and kept the birds from eating it.

Just as the sun was going down, God made Abram fall asleep. In his dream, Abram felt afraid, but God said, "Your great-grandchildren and their children's children will live in another land, where they will be slaves for four hundred years. But I will bring them out of that land, and they will be rich. Your great-grandchildren's great-grandchildren will come back here to the land I have shown you."

The sun had gone down and it was growing dark when Abram saw flames and smoke passing between the pieces of meat he had laid out. Then the Lord made a covenant with Abram. God told Abram, "I will give you all this land for many miles in each direction."

Sarah and Abraham

Genesis 16, 17, and 18;
Augmented by verses from Genesis 11, 12, 13, and 23

Sarai was Abram's wife. She went with him from their home in Ur to
Haran. Later she went many more miles with Abram. They went together to
Canaan, where God told them to go.

Sarai and Abram went to a valley in Egypt for a time, because they needed
better pastures for their animals. When they came back, they pitched their
tents in the shade of the sacred trees of Mamre at Hebron. By then she was
getting older. All this time Sarai had wanted children, but none had come.

In those days a man could have more than one wife, but Abram had
married only Sarai. One day she told Abram, "We have no children. You may
also marry my maid, Hagar. Maybe she can have a son for us."

Abram did what Sarai said, and soon Hagar was expecting a baby. Hagar
began to treat Sarai rudely, because Hagar was going to have a child and
Sarai had none. So Sarai became angry, and Hagar ran away.

Hagar nearly died of thirst in the desert. God came to her and told her to
return to Sarai. God showed Hagar a well of water so that she would not die.
Hagar went back home and had a son named Ishmael.

When Abram was an old man, God came to him and said, "I am God
Almighty. We will make a covenant. You and your children's children will
have this land forever." Then God changed Abram's name to Abraham and
Sarai's name to Sarah. Then God said, "Sarah will have a son."

"Sarah is ninety years old," said Abraham. "Can't my son Ishmael be the one to have your blessing?"

"Ishmael will be the father of twelve princes, but Sarah's son will be the one to carry on our covenant."

One day several years later, Abraham was sitting by the trees outside his tent. Three men or angels came to him and asked for food. Abraham told Sarah, "Quick! Get your best flour and make some bread." Then he had the servants fix some meat. He got some cheese and milk. He put all these things out so the visitors could eat.

One of them said, "Where is Sarah?"

"She is in her tent," Abraham said.

"I will return in the springtime," said the visitor. "After that, Sarah will have a son."

Sarah was in her tent. She heard what the visitor said and started to laugh, because she was more than ninety years old. She knew she was too old to have a baby.

"Who ever heard of a woman as old as I am having a baby?" she said.

God spoke to Abraham. "Why did Sarah laugh?" God asked.

"I didn't laugh," said Sarah, because she knew she should not laugh at God.

"Yes, you did," God said.

The next spring Sarah had the baby God promised to her and to Abraham, even though they were old. The baby was named Isaac, which means "laughing."

"God has given me a reason to laugh," she said. "Everyone who hears of an old woman like me having a baby will laugh. Who would have believed this? But at last we have a son!"

Sarah lived to be a hundred and twenty-seven years old.

Jacob Becomes Israel

Genesis 25:20–34; 32:3–21;
Augmented by verses from Genesis 27, 29, and 31

Abraham's son, Isaac, grew up and married his beautiful cousin, Rebekah. They had twin sons, Esau and Jacob.

When Isaac was old and blind, Jacob tricked his father into giving him his blessing and promising that he would be more important than his brother Esau. Then Jacob was afraid Esau would try to kill him, so he ran away to Haran, where he had cousins and aunts and uncles.

In those days a man could have more than one wife, so Jacob married two of his cousins, Leah and Rachel. He worked for their father, Laban, for many years.

Finally Jacob told his wives and his eleven sons and his daughter Dinah and all their servants to get ready to leave. They loaded their tents and all the things they owned on camels. They got their flocks of sheep and goats and their herds of cattle. Then they started for Canaan.

Jacob sent one of his helpers with a message to his brother, Esau, that he wanted to be friends. He was still afraid that Esau might try to harm him or kill his animals.

Then Jacob got word that his brother Esau was coming to meet him. He heard that Esau was bringing four hundred men. And he was afraid.

Jacob prayed. "God of Abraham and my father, Isaac, you told me to return to this land," he said. "I am afraid that my brother, Esau, will kill me.

But you have told me that you will do good for me. Remember that you have promised to make my children and grandchildren as many as the grains of sands in the ocean, which I can't count."

Then Jacob sent many sheep and goats and cows to Esau as a present. In the middle of the night he sent his wives and his two maids and his children across a creek called Jabbok. This creek was the border of Esau's land.

After the family and everything Jacob owned was across the stream, he was left alone. A strange man came to Jacob, and they fought and wrestled all night. When the sun was coming up, the man hit Jacob on his leg and pulled it out of joint.

Jacob still hung on to the man. "I will not let you go unless you bless me."

"What is your name?" asked the man.

"Jacob," he answered.

"Your name is not Jacob any more," said the man. "Your name will be Israel now. The name *Israel* means "someone who wrestles with God."

"What is your name?" asked Jacob.

The man said, "That is a foolish question." He gave Jacob a blessing.

Jacob said, "I will call this place Peniel. This word means 'the face of God.' I have seen God face to face, and I did not die!"

Then Jacob, now called Israel, went into Canaan and made friends with his twin brother, Esau. Later they went together to see their father, Isaac, who was now a very old man. Israel and Rebekah and their children became a great family.

Joseph Becomes a Slave

Genesis 37 and 39;
Augmented by verses from Genesis 35

Jacob, whose name was changed to Israel, had twelve sons. Their names were Reuben, Simeon, Levi, Judah, Issachar, Zebulun, Dan, Naphtali, Gad, Asher, Joseph, and Benjamin.

Joseph's father loved him more than all his other sons. When Joseph was seventeen, Israel gave him a beautiful coat with long sleeves. Joseph's big brothers became angry because their father loved Joseph best, and they had trouble speaking to him without fighting.

Joseph had a dream, and he said to his brothers, "Listen to the dream I had! I dreamed we were tying up bundles of wheat in the field," he said. "My bundle stood up straight, but your bundles all bowed down to mine."

The brothers were angry. "Do you think you're a king, so we have to bow to you?" they asked.

Then Joseph had another dream. He told his father and brothers, "I dreamed that the sun and the moon and eleven stars all bowed down to me."

"Joseph, what is this?" said Israel. "Should your mother and I and your brothers all bow down to you?" The brothers were very angry and jealous, but their father always remembered Joseph's dream.

One day Israel sent Joseph up to the hill country near Shechem. "Your brothers are up there with the sheep and goats," he said. "Go see if everything is all right, and come back to tell me."

Joseph went to those fields, but he found out that his brothers had gone to Dothan.

His brothers saw him coming. "Here comes that dreamer," said one of them. "Let's get rid of him. Let's kill him and throw him in a pit. We can say that a wild animal killed him."

"Don't hurt him," said Reuben, the oldest son. "Just throw him in the pit." Reuben was planning to come get Joseph out of the pit later.

They took Joseph's fine coat and threw him in the pit. Then they saw people going to Egypt with many camels. They sold Joseph to them as a slave for twenty pieces of silver.

Reuben was not there when they sold his brother. When he came back to help Joseph out of the pit, he was very upset to find him gone.

His brothers took Joseph's coat, dipped it in the blood of a goat, and showed it to their father.

"A wild animal must have killed him!" his father said. Israel was very sad for many years, because he thought Joseph was dead. But Joseph was alive in Egypt, the slave of an army captain named Potiphar.

God was with Joseph, and soon Potiphar noticed that everything Joseph did turned out well. He put Joseph in charge of his house, and he let him take care of some of his business. As soon as Potiphar did this, God blessed him, and Potiphar got very rich. So Potiphar let Joseph take charge of all his business.

But Potiphar's wife got angry with Joseph, and she persuaded Potiphar to put Joseph in prison. But God took care of Joseph. Soon the prison keeper had Joseph watching the other prisoners and deciding what work would be done. He stopped worrying about any prison business because he knew he could trust Joseph.

Joseph and the Meaning of Dreams
Genesis 40:1–41:45

One day the butler and the baker from the king's palace in Egypt were put in prison. This was the same prison where Joseph, the son of Israel, was put by Potiphar. The prison keeper let Joseph take charge of the butler and baker, because he trusted Joseph to help him.

One morning the butler and baker both said they had dreams they could not understand. They were upset because they did not understand their dreams.

"The meaning of dreams comes from God," Joseph told them. He listened to their dreams and explained them. He told the butler, "Your dream was a happy one. You will end up as the king's favorite server." He told the baker, "Your dream is not so happy. You will end up in terrible trouble with the king."

Both these dreams came true. The butler meant to reward Joseph, but he forgot about him for two years.

However, one day Pharaoh, the king of Egypt, had dreams he did not understand. Then Pharaoh's butler remembered Joseph, and Pharaoh sent for him.

"I have dreamed about seven fat cows and seven thin ones," Pharaoh told Joseph. "The seven very thin cows ate up the fat cows. And I dreamed about seven fat ears of corn and seven thin ones."

"God has told in these dreams what will happen and what you must do," Joseph told Pharaoh. "There will be seven years of good harvest, with plenty of food for everyone. Then there will be seven years without good crops. Everyone will starve unless you save grain from the seven good harvests."

Then Joseph said, "Because you dreamed about this in two ways, once about cows and once about corn, we know God will make this happen soon. Pharaoh, you should get someone who is very wise and honest and have him save grain for the thin years."

Pharaoh said, "This is a good idea. And where would we find a man any better than you to do this job?"

So Pharaoh made Joseph his chief helper. He gave him a ring from his own hand. He gave him clothes a king could wear and a gold chain to wear around his neck. Joseph rode in the second best chariot in the land, and when he went by, people had to bow to him. Joseph married a rich Egyptian woman named Asenath. He went out to all of Egypt and collected grain in the seven good years.

Joseph Forgives His Brothers

Genesis 41:41–46:7

Although Joseph's brothers had sold him as a slave, God took care of him. He was no longer a slave but was now the governor of Egypt.

Joseph knew there would be seven years when the farms would do well and seven years they would do poorly. During the seven years of plenty he put a fifth of each farm's crop in storehouses for the seven years of hunger that were coming.

After the seven years of plenty, seven years of hunger began. Everyone in Egypt was starving and cried to the king.

"You must see Joseph," Pharaoh told them. "Do whatever he tells you." So Joseph opened up all the storehouses and sold grain to the Egyptians. Soon people came from many other countries to buy grain, because there was hunger in those countries, too.

Joseph's father (Israel, who used to be called Jacob) heard that there was food in Egypt. He did not know that Joseph was there. So Joseph's ten older brothers went to Egypt to buy grain, but they left the youngest brother, Benjamin, with their father. None of them knew that Joseph was the governor in Egypt.

When the brothers came to the palace, they bowed to Joseph so their faces touched the ground. They did not know who he was, and Joseph pretended not to know them.

"I think you are spies from another country," he said.

"No, sir," they answered. "Our father sent us to buy food. We are all from the same family. Benjamin, our youngest brother, is still at home."

Joseph pretended not to believe them. He put them in prison for three days. Then he said, "You bring your youngest brother back here, so I can see if you are telling the truth. I will keep one of you, Simeon, here until you come back."

The brothers talked to each other and said, "This is because of what we did to Joseph. Now we are being punished." They said this in their Hebrew language, and Joseph pretended not to understand them. But when they were not looking, he cried.

Then Joseph told servants to fill up the grain sacks of his brothers and to put the money they had paid into the sacks, too. When they got to their home in Canaan, they found their money. They were very frightened. They wondered if the governor thought they had cheated him.

"The governor says we must take Benjamin with us if we want to see Simeon again," they told their father. They told him everything that had happened in Egypt.

For many months Joseph's father and brothers and their wives and children ate bread made from the grain they bought in Egypt. But finally it was all gone. Their father said, "You must go to Egypt again to buy a little food."

Judah said, "We must take Benjamin, or the governor will not talk to us."

Israel said, "Joseph is dead. Now I have lost Simeon. On top of that, you want to take Benjamin away, too."

They argued with their father for a long time. Israel finally said, "It must be. You may take Benjamin and go. But take the governor a gift of some of our honey and nuts and spices, and maybe he will be kind to us. Pray that God lets me see Benjamin and Simeon again."

So the brothers went back to Egypt and took Benjamin with them. When Joseph saw Benjamin, he told his servants to make a feast. He asked the brothers questions about their home and their father. Then he told his servants to fill their grain sacks, put the money they had paid into the sacks, and put his favorite silver cup in Benjamin's sack.

When the brothers were on their way to Canaan, Joseph sent guards to bring them back. "Why did you steal from me?" he asked. He pretended to be very angry. "Now Benjamin must stay here as my slave," he said.

"My lord, our father is a very old man. He has already lost one son. If we go back without Benjamin, he will die. Keep me as your slave instead," begged Judah.

Joseph could not stand any more. He sent all the servants out. He burst into tears. When he could talk, he said, "I am Joseph! Tell me, is our father really still alive?"

At first Joseph's brothers did not understand. Then Joseph said, "Come close to me and look. I am Joseph, the brother you sold as a slave. It was God who planned this. God sent me here so I could save your lives. So hurry back to Canaan and tell our father that God has made me governor of all Egypt." Then Joseph threw his arms around his brother Benjamin and cried.

The king of Egypt heard that these were Joseph's brothers and said, "Bring your family here and I will give them food and land."

So they went back and told their father, "We have found Joseph! He is alive and is governor of all Egypt!"

At first Israel did not believe them, but finally he did. "My son Joseph is alive. I must go to see him," he said.

Israel prayed to God, and God said, "Do not be afraid to go to Egypt. I will be with you. And I will make your children into a great nation."

So all the brothers took their wives and children, their servants and cattle and sheep and goats and wagons to Egypt. At last Israel saw all twelve of his sons together.

The Birth of Moses

Exodus 1:1–2:10

While Joseph was governor of Egypt, Israel and his twelve sons came there to live with their families and servants and animals. There were seventy people in the family of Israel who came to Egypt, not counting the servants. Soon more children were born, and the family grew and grew.

When Joseph was very old, he died. His big family was treated well by the Egyptians, because they remembered what Joseph had done for them.

After nearly four hundred years, a new king came to Egypt who did not know about Joseph. He said, "Now there are hundreds and thousands of these Hebrew people of Israel. They are becoming too powerful. If Egypt goes to war, these Hebrews might join our enemies."

The king made the Hebrews work as slaves. All day these people had to do the hardest jobs in all Egypt. Some had to make bricks out of mud and straw. Others worked in the fields. They were not treated well by the men who were in charge of slaves.

The king of Egypt was still not happy. He talked to two of the Hebrew midwives. These are women who help when babies are born.

"When Hebrew boy babies are born, you must kill them," said Pharaoh the king. "But if girls are born, you may let them live."

But these women believed in God, and they would not do what Pharaoh said.

"Why are there so many Hebrew boys?" Pharaoh asked. "I told you to kill all the boy babies."

"The Hebrew women are very strong," said the midwives. "Their babies are born before we get there."

Then Pharaoh said to everyone in Egypt, "When you see any little Hebrew boy babies, you must throw them into the Nile River."

Now there were a man and his wife from the family of Levi. They had a baby boy, and they hid him in their house until he was three months old. When he was too big to hide, his mother took a big basket and painted it with pitch to keep the water out. She put the baby into the basket and let it float in the reeds by the river's edge.

The baby's sister stood where she could see what would happen to him. Soon she saw Pharaoh's daughter. This princess of Egypt came down to the river to swim with her maids. She saw the basket and had one of her maids pull it out of the water.

When the princess opened the basket, she saw the baby inside, crying, and she felt sorry for him.

"This is one of those poor Hebrew children," she said.

Then the baby's sister ran up. "Should I find a Hebrew woman to take care of the baby?" she asked.

"Yes, go!" said Pharaoh's daughter.

Soon the little girl came back with the baby's own mother.

"Please feed this baby and take care of him until he is older," the princess told her. "I will pay you to take care of him." So the baby's mother took him home. When he was a big boy, she took him back to the princess.

The princess adopted the boy for her own son. She named him Moses, a name that means "out of the water."

Moses and the Burning Bush

Exodus 2, 3, and 4

When Moses was a boy, he was adopted by Pharaoh's daughter and grew up in her house. But when he was a man, he wanted to know his own Hebrew people better.

One day, when he was walking around the city, he saw an Egyptian beating one of the Hebrews. Moses killed the Egyptian. Then he ran away and went to live in Midian, another country, because he was afraid of Pharaoh.

Moses married a woman in Midian. Her name was Zipporah. Moses tended her father's sheep. Moses and Zipporah had one son, whose name was Gershom.

One day, when Moses was out with the sheep on a mountain, he saw a bush on fire. He watched it, and an angel from God appeared in the flames. The bush kept on burning but did not burn up.

"How can this be?" he wondered. He went to have a closer look at this wonderful sight.

When God saw that Moses was stopping to see the burning bush, God called, "Moses, Moses!"

"Here I am," said Moses.

"Do not come any closer to the fire," God said. Take off your shoes, because the place where you are standing is a holy place."

Then God said, "I am the God of Abraham and Isaac and Jacob." And Moses hid his face because he was afraid to look at God.

God spoke to Moses from the burning bush and said, "I have heard the prayers of the Hebrew children of Israel. I know they are slaves. I know that they are treated cruelly by their masters. I will rescue them and take them out of Egypt to a good land. I will take them to Canaan, a land of milk and honey. Come, Moses. I will send you to Pharaoh, king of Egypt, to get my people out of Egypt."

"People will not believe me," said Moses.

But the Lord said, "I will be with you."

Then Moses asked, "Who shall I say sent me?"

And God said, "Tell the people that you are sent by I AM, the God of Abraham and Isaac and Jacob."

Moses argued with God and said, "I stammer when I talk. People will not listen."

God replied, "Who is it that made people able to speak?" But Moses still argued.

God was angry with Moses and said, "Your brother Aaron is a good speaker. He will speak for you."

And so Moses and Aaron went back to Egypt.

The Plagues and Passover
Exodus 5–12

The Hebrew people of Israel were slaves in Egypt. They were doing a lot of hard work for Pharaoh, and he didn't want them to stop. So when Moses and Aaron spoke to Pharaoh, he wouldn't let the people of Israel go to Canaan. Moses showed Pharaoh many miracles of God, but Pharaoh's magicians could do miracles, too.

After Moses and Aaron went to Pharaoh, the Hebrews were treated worse than ever. "Leave us alone!" they said to Moses and Aaron. "You have turned Pharaoh against us!"

God told Moses that he had to go back to Pharaoh.

Nine times Moses went to Pharaoh and said, "Let my people go."

Nine times Pharaoh did not let the people go.

God sent nine plagues to Egypt. God let Moses turn the Nile River to blood. Then God sent thousands of frogs, and then gnats, and then great swarms of flies.

When each plague came, Pharaoh said, "Ask your God to take this plague away, and I will let you go." But when the plague was gone, Pharaoh became stubborn and said, "I will not let your people go."

Soon there were plagues of sickness in the Egyptian cattle, and many cows died. After that there were plagues of skin diseases on people and of terrible hail that smashed the crops. The locusts ate every tree and plant that was left standing after the hail. And after that there were three days of darkness.

When each plague came, Pharaoh said, "Ask your God to take this away, and I will let you go." But when the plague was gone, Pharaoh became stubborn and said, "I will not let your people go."

Finally God told Moses, "Now I will send the most terrible thing of all. The oldest child of every Egyptian family will die. The oldest of every family of animals will die. Grown men who are their parents' oldest will die."

Then God told Moses, "But your people will not die. Each family must kill a lamb to eat for dinner. You must mark the door of each house of the Hebrews with the blood of the lamb. The Lord will pass over your houses and your people will be safe. Then Pharaoh will let you go."

The people did as God said, and the oldest child of every Egyptian house died. But none of the Hebrew people died.

Pharaoh said, "Take these people and get out of Egypt. We can't stand any more plagues from your God."

The Hebrew people loaded up all their belongings in a hurry. They even took the bread they were making without removing it from the bowls. When they baked it, it was flat because they hadn't put leaven in it yet.

God spoke to Moses and Aaron. "In the new land I am giving you," God said, "you will celebrate my Passover. This month will always be the first month of the year for you. Every year, you will mark the two doorposts of your houses and the beam over the doorway with the blood of the Passover lamb."

God told them that they should roast the lamb and eat it for dinner. God told them also to serve flat, unleavened bread with the dinner.

"You must eat this meal dressed for traveling, with your walking stick in your hand and your shoes on your feet," God told them.

God said that when their children who were born in Canaan asked why they kept this service, they must tell them, "It is the sacrifice of the Lord's Passover, because God passed over our houses when the Egyptians died."

God said to the people, "You must do this every year, you and your children and your children's children and their children. This Passover must be observed every year forever and ever."

When the Hebrew people of Israel heard these things, they bowed their heads and worshiped God.

Crossing the Red Sea

Exodus 14:1–15:21

When Pharaoh knew that the Hebrew people of Israel had finally left Egypt, he suddenly changed his mind. So did many other people in that country.

"What have we done?" they cried. "We can't get along without our Hebrew slaves and workers!"

So the king took his army and chariots and began to chase after the people of Israel. The fastest horses and chariots caught up with them where they were camped on the beach by the Red Sea.

The people of Israel looked up and saw Pharaoh and his army coming after them. God had sent a pillar of cloud to lead them, and now they cried out to God. They shouted to Moses, "Wasn't there room to bury us in Egypt? Did you have to bring us out here in the wilderness to die? We told you a long time ago to leave us alone at our jobs in Egypt. We would have been better off staying there!"

Moses told them, "Don't be afraid! Stay where you are, and the Lord will save us."

God said to Moses, "What is all this crying? Tell the people to get up and march. Stretch out your hand over the sea."

Early in the morning, Moses stretched out his hand over the sea. A great wind came up and changed the sea bed into dry land.

All the people of Israel walked on a dry path with water on both sides. When the Egyptian soldiers saw what was happening, they went after them. But the wheels of the Egyptian chariots stuck in the sand.

God told Moses, "Now stretch your hand out over the sea again." Moses did that, and the waters came back and drowned all the Egyptian soldiers who were chasing the people of Israel. But none of the people of Israel were harmed. After this, the people believed in the Lord God and in God's servant, Moses.

Aaron spoke what Moses heard God say. Their sister Miriam became a prophet. (This is a name for someone who hears what God says and tells others.)

After Moses stretched out his hand and God sent a wind to get the people safely across the Red Sea, everyone celebrated. Miriam jumped up on the beach and grabbed a tambourine. All the women followed her with bells and tambourines as she sang and danced. The song she sang had these words: "I will sing to the Lord, for God is the winner in a wonderful way! God has thrown horses and their riders into the sea!"

Manna and Quails

Exodus 15:22–16:36;
Augmented by verses from Numbers 11

After the people of Israel crossed the Red Sea on dry land, they camped for three days and ran out of water. They came to a pond in the desert called Marah.

The people began to get angry at Moses because the water of Marah was too bitter. God showed Moses a certain kind of log to throw into the water, which made the water good to drink.

They camped at a place called Elim, with many springs and palm trees, and they went on from there. About two months after they left Egypt, they were running out of food.

"We wish we were back in Egypt!" the people shouted at Moses. "It would be better if God had killed us back there where we had our pots of stew and plenty of bread to eat. Out here we're slowly dying of hunger."

God told Moses, "I will send bread down from heaven like rain. Every day the people will gather enough to eat for that day. On the sixth day they will pick up enough for the seventh day. On the seventh day everyone must rest."

So in the mornings they gathered the bread that God sent like rain. It was in flakes, like snow. The people made it into loaves, or they cooked it like cereal. They called it manna. (This sounded like the Hebrew word that means "what is it?")

Then they began to crave other things. "Remember in Egypt when we had fresh fish and lemons and cucumbers? Remember the onions and garlic and melons? We're getting weak now, and all we have to eat is this same old manna."

So God said, "In the morning you will eat manna, and in the evening you will eat meat." That evening a flock of birds called quails rested in the desert. The people of Israel caught them in nets and roasted them, and so they had meat.

Moses told the people, "Now God has fed you. We will keep a jar of manna forever, so that our children and their children will remember forever that God fed us."

The people of Israel ate manna in the desert for the whole forty years they lived there.

Water from the Rock

Exodus 17:1–7

The people were no longer starving, because God sent them manna every morning and quails to catch and roast in the evening. But after a while they ran out of water. While they were camping at a place called Rephidim, the people became angry with Moses again. "Give us water!" they shouted.

"Why are you shouting at me?" Moses asked them. "Why don't you trust God? You are testing God again."

But the people were so thirsty that they got angrier. "Why didn't you leave us in Egypt?" they cried. "Why didn't you leave us there? Did you bring us out here so we and our children and our cattle would all die of thirst?"

Moses cried out to God, "These people are about ready to kill me. What should I do?"

God told Moses, "Walk out in front of the people. Take some of the leaders with you. Take the rod that you held out over the Nile River and go to Mount Horeb. I will be there, and you will strike a rock, and water will come out of it."

Moses did what God said. He brought some of the elders, or leaders, of the people of Israel with him, and he went to the bottom of the mountain. He struck a rock with his rod, and water came pouring out of it for the people to drink.

Moses called the place where the rock gave water two names. He called it Massah, which means "proof," because the people asked God for proof again. He also called it Meribah, which means "argument," because the people of Israel argued and fought with him about the water and about nearly everything that happened on the desert.

The Ten Commandments
Exodus 19, 20, and 25

The people of Israel were traveling through the desert on the way to Canaan, the land that God had promised them.

Almost three months after they left Egypt, they camped near a mountain called Sinai. Moses went up on the mountain. God told him, "Tell the people of Israel that they have seen all I did to make you safe and free from Egypt. In three days I am going to make a great covenant with you. The people of Israel will always be my chosen people, if they keep my covenant."

Moses told the people what God said. He told all the people to pray and wash their clothes to be ready to hear God's plan for them. "God will give us the covenant from a thick cloud," he told them.

On the third day there was thunder and lightning on top of the mountain. The people heard the sound of a trumpet growing louder and louder. God was on the mountain with fire and smoke and clouds, and there was an earthquake.

God told Moses to bring his brother Aaron up on the mountain and to let the people stay behind. "My power will be too great for them to see and hear," God said.

These are the ten commandments of the covenant that God told Moses:

"I am the Lord, your God. I brought you out of Egypt. Do not worship any other gods besides me.

"Do not make any statues or pictures or carvings of anyone in heaven or on earth or in the sea. Do not bow down to any statues or pictures or worship them. If you hate me and disobey me, you and your children and grandchildren and great-grandchildren will have great trouble. But I will show my love forever to those who love me and keep my commandments.

"Do not use the name of God without respect.

"Remember the sabbath day, to keep it holy. Work six days. But every seventh day is a sabbath day. It is holy. Rest and do no work. Your sons and daughters and servants and animals should not work on the sabbath. The Lord made heaven and the earth and the sea and all that is in them in six days, and on the seventh day God rested. The Lord has blessed the sabbath day and made it holy.

"Respect your father and mother, so you may live a long time in the promised land.

"Do not kill.

"Do not be unfaithful to your husband or wife.

"Do not steal.

"Do not lie about other people.

"Do not envy what other people have. Do not wish for their houses or their wives or their servants or their animals or anything that your neighbors have."

These commandments were carved on two sacred stone tablets. After giving Moses the ten commandments, God told him how to make an altar, an ark, or special wooden box for the stone tablets, and a tent of worship.

The Golden Calf

Exodus 32:1–34;
Augmented by verses from Exodus 20 and 24

While Moses was on the mountain talking with God about the covenant and the ten commandments, his brother Aaron stayed in camp with the people.

"We are afraid of the smoke and fire and thunder," the people had told Moses. "You speak to God for us and tell us what God says."

So Moses stayed in the thick cloud on the mountain while the people waited. He was on the mountain for forty days. The people got tired of waiting and went to Aaron.

"Make us gods that we can see and bow down to," they said. "We don't know what has happened to Moses. He brought us out here in the desert and then disappeared."

Aaron said, "Collect all your gold earrings." So they all took off their gold earrings. Aaron melted the gold and made a statue of a golden calf.

"Here," he told the people. "Here is your god. This is the one who brought you from Egypt."

"Tomorrow will be a feast day to honor God," Aaron said.

When the people saw the calf, they gave offerings to it. They had a feast and danced and sang.

Up on the mountain God spoke to Moses. "Get down there," God told Moses. "The people are in trouble. They have made a golden calf, and they are bowing and praying to it. They are saying that this calf brought them out of Egypt."

Moses listened as God went on. "These people are stubborn," God told him. "I had better destroy them and start a new people, with you as the father of them all."

"Lord, do not hurt them!" Moses cried. "Then the Egyptians will say that the God of the people of Israel just took them out in the desert to kill them. Remember your promise to Abraham and Isaac and Israel that the land you are giving us is for their families forever."

So God decided not to destroy all the people of Israel.

Moses started down the mountain. He took with him the two stone tablets that the ten commandments were written on. Part way down he was joined by Joshua, who was a captain of the Israelites.

Soon they heard the sound of loud voices in the camp below them. "That sounds like the people are fighting a war with someone," Joshua said.

But Moses said, "That isn't the sound of shouting and battle. It is the sound of singing."

When they came into camp, they saw the golden calf and the people dancing around it. Moses was so angry that he threw down the stone tablets that God had given him and broke them to pieces. Then he took the golden calf that Aaron and the people had made and burned it. He ground it into powder, put the powdered gold into water, and made the people drink it.

Moses told Aaron, "You have helped make the people do something very wrong. Why did you do this?"

"They wanted me to make them a god," Aaron told Moses. "So we melted down their earrings in the fire, and out came this calf."

"Whoever is on God's side, stand by me!" Moses shouted. All the people from the family of Levi came to stand by Moses. They took swords and killed the people who worshiped the golden calf.

The next day, Moses went back up the mountain. "What the people did was terrible," he told God. "But I beg you to forgive them. If you can't forgive them, then be angry at me, not at them."

"I will have to punish these people for their sins," God said. "But you must go on and lead them to Canaan. I will send an angel with you."

The Face of Moses Shines

Exodus 34:1–2, 28–35;
Augmented by verses from Exodus 32, 33, and 35

When Moses saw the golden calf that the people worshiped, he threw down the stone tablets with the ten commandments on them. Afterward he went back up the mountain and begged God to forgive the people and lead them to the promised land.

"I will do this, because I am faithful to my promises," God told him. Then God said, "Cut two more tablets out of stone, like the ones I gave you. Early tomorrow morning come up here on the mountain alone."

God told Moses what to write on the stone tablets. When Moses came down from the mountain with the two stone tablets in his hands, he did not know that the skin on his face was shining.

Aaron and the people looked at Moses and were afraid. They wouldn't come near him. Finally Moses called out to them. Then Aaron and the other leaders of the people came and spoke with him.

After that, the rest of the people came close, so that he could tell them about the ten commandments that God had given him on Mount Sinai.

When Moses was through telling these things, he put a cloth over his face.

God's Law for Israel

Deuteronomy 5:29–6:9

Moses talked to the Hebrew people of Israel about the law that God gave them. "Remember that God brought us out of Egypt, and is going to give us our promised land," Moses told the people.

Then he told them, "Listen, Israel! Listen, everyone! The Lord is our God, the Lord alone. You must love the Lord your God with all your heart, and with all your soul, and with all your strength!"

Moses reminded the people that they should keep God's law in their hearts. "Teach this law to your children," he told them. "Talk about it everywhere, at home and away from home."

Then he told them that God wanted them to think of the law when they went to bed at night and when they got up in the morning.

"Write the law on pieces of leather, and tie them on your arms and wear them for headbands," Moses said. "Write the law of Israel on your gates. Write it on the posts of your front doors."

The People Complain to Moses
Numbers 11

There came a time when the people of Israel complained to the Lord and to each other about their troubles in the wilderness. To make things worse, some strangers from the desert joined with the people of Israel in their camps. These people were very greedy for good things, and they made the people of Israel think about food and cry even more.

"Oh, we wish we had some meat!" they cried. "In Egypt, we had plenty of fish. There were cucumbers and watermelons. There were leeks and onions. There was garlic to flavor our food. But all we see here is manna, manna, manna! We're tired of it!"

The manna that God sent from heaven looked like small seeds. The people gathered it up and ground it into flour. Then they made cakes that tasted like bread. Every night the manna fell when the dew came.

Moses heard the people who stood in the doorways of their tents, complaining about food. The Lord became angry, and Moses felt unhappy.

"Why have you done this to me?" he asked God. "I have tried to do everything you asked. Now the people are mad because they want different food. Am I their mother? Am I supposed to feed them and rock them to sleep?"

Moses thought for a while, and then he went on praying to God. "Where can I find meat for all these people? Lord, I can't take care of everyone by myself. If you want me to do it alone, then kill me."

God answered Moses and told him what to do. "Get seventy elders of the people. They shall bear some of the burden with you."

Moses had the seventy stand around the tent of God. Then God spoke to them from a cloud of glory. For the first time, they were allowed to share part of the spirit that the Lord gave Moses.

A strong wind blew thousands of quails all around the camp. People spent two days and a night collecting them.

The Tabernacle
Exodus 35–40

After Moses gave the people the ten commandments, he explained that they must keep one day each week to rest and worship God. "You may work for six days every week, but on the seventh day you will rest and worship God. This will be called sabbath. It is the Lord's day. You may not do any work or even make a fire for cooking on that day."

Then Moses told them that God wanted them to make a tabernacle, a place for worship. This would be a special large tent that could be moved. Inside the tabernacle there would be an altar and a holy place holding the ark of the covenant.

An ark is a box or chest. A man named Bezalel, who knew how to build beautiful things, made most of this ark. The ark was made of fine wood and covered with pure gold. It had gold-covered poles for carrying it. Inside the ark were placed the stone tablets with the ten commandments.

Moses told the people, "God wants you to give your finest things to make this holy tabernacle. Bring gold or silver, fine blue, purple, or bright red cloth or thread. Bring wool yarn, leather, fine wood, oil for the lamps, and spices to make incense or perfumed oil. If you have jewels, bring them to make the special things a priest will wear."

The people thought about the things Moses told them, and they felt excited. They brought all the things that he had asked for.

There were lampstands, which were tall gold candleholders with flowers carved in them. The people hung curtains made of embroidered cloth and leather and fur skins for a wall around the tabernacle. The curtains were hung by blue loops, and held tightly together with gold and bronze clasps.

Inside the curtains was a large space, many feet long and wide. An altar was made for incense, and another one for burning animals that were given for God. There were tables for the special bread that was given to God.

The ark of the covenant was placed inside a small tent of its own called the most holy place. Only once a year did the priests go into the most holy place. The priests were people from the families of Levi, and Aaron was their leader.

When the tabernacle was set up on the first of the month, with the tent covering over it, Moses burned incense and put all the things inside it. In all their journeys, when the people of Israel set up the tabernacle, they could see God's cloud by day and God's fire by night.

Spies in the Promised Land
Numbers 13 and 14

When Moses and the people of Israel got to the borders of Canaan, God told Moses to pick leaders from each of the twelve tribes of Israel.

"Send these men into the land I have promised you to spy out the country," God said.

Moses picked twelve men. "Go beyond the Negev desert, and see what the land is like," Moses told them. "See how many people live there and how strong they are. Come back and tell us whether there are trees, and bring us some of the fruit."

The twelve men went to the Negev, and then to Hebron, where Abraham once lived. They found that tribes with many big men had moved into Hebron.

This was the time when the grapes of this country were just ripe. So they went to a valley and cut a branch with a huge bunch of grapes on it, and two of the men carried it on a pole between them. They also picked figs and pomegranates.

When the twelve came back from Canaan, they stood in front of everyone in the camp and showed them the fruit of the promised land.

"We went into Canaan and found that it is full of good milk and honey and plenty of fruit," they said. "But the land we saw is full of huge men, giants, who made us look and feel as small as grasshoppers."

The people of Israel shouted and cried all night. They all said, "Oh, if only we had stayed in Egypt! It would have been better to live as slaves than to be killed out here in the desert. We want to go back to Egypt."

When they heard this, Moses and Aaron fell on the ground and hid their faces. Then Joshua, one of the spies, stood up with Caleb. They were so angry at the people that they tore their clothes and shouted, "The land we saw was good! If the Lord is with us, he will give us the land. Do not rebel against the Lord."

But the people of Israel would not listen. Suddenly God's shining glory filled the Tabernacle. All the people saw it. God called out and said, "Moses, how long will these people insult me? What more do they want, after all the miracles I have done for them?"

But Moses begged God not to kill the Israelites. "Please, Lord," he said, "forgive them for this, just as you have forgiven them for everything since we left Egypt."

Then God said, "I will not kill them, because you have asked me, Moses. But listen to this. These people saw my glory, both in Egypt and in the desert, and still they turn against me. Tomorrow you will turn and go into the desert lands near the Red Sea. You will stay in the desert for years, until everyone who is now twenty years old or more is dead, except for Caleb and Joshua. These two wanted to obey me, so they will live to go into Canaan."

The next day the people were sorry. "We will go into the promised land right now," they said. "We were wrong and disobeyed God, when we said we would not go."

Moses said, "Are you trying to disobey God again? God will not protect you now. It is too late."

Some people did not listen. They went into Canaan, and tribes who lived there chased them out of the land.

As for the rest of the people of Israel, they lived in the desert for forty more years before they could go into the land God had promised them.

Joshua Crosses the Jordan

Joshua 1:1–4:20;
Augmented by verses from Deuteronomy 32 and 34

After the people of Israel spent forty years in the desert, God told Moses to climb a high hill to see the land promised them.

Moses looked out from the top of a mountain. He could see the large, good land of Canaan across the Jordan River below. He knew his children and grandchildren and great-grandchildren and their children's children would live there and be happy.

Moses put his hands on Joshua's head to show that God was now giving command to Joshua. Then Moses went away into the desert and died. He was one hundred and twenty years old, but he was as strong as a young man until he died.

The people of Israel spent thirty days remembering Moses and all he had done for them. Then God called Joshua and said, "Joshua, Moses is gone. Now you must lead the people across the Jordan River into Canaan. Be strong and brave. You will be the one to help these people have the land that I have promised. Do not be afraid of the people of the country, because I am the Lord and I will be with you."

Joshua sent two secret spies into the country. "Go look over the land," he told them. "Especially look at the city of Jericho."

When the two men arrived in Jericho, they met a woman named Rahab. While they were staying at her house, the king of Jericho said, "I hear that two men of Israel are in Jericho as spies." He sent a message to Rahab that said, "Send those men of Israel to me. They are spies for the armies of Israel."

Rahab told the two spies, "I have heard of the people of Israel, and of your God. I will help you, if you ask your God to save me and my family when Joshua comes."

She hid the men under some straw on her roof and told the king she did not know where they were. Later, she let them out her window by a rope, and they went back to Joshua to report.

"Watch for a house with a bright red cord tied to the window," the men told Joshua. "That is the house of Rahab, who helped us. We promised that we would not hurt her or her family."

Early in the morning Joshua and all the people got ready to cross the Jordan River. His captains went through the camp shouting, "When you see the priests carrying the ark of the covenant, follow it."

God told Joshua, "From this day on I will speak to you as I did to Moses. Now tell the people that they will know that the living God is with them. When the ark is at the edge of the water, the river will stop running until everyone is across."

The priests carrying the ark stepped into the water. The river stopped flowing, just as God had said. The priests stopped halfway across, and the people went over the Jordan on dry land. Twelve captains each took a big rock from the place where the priests stood. When everyone was across, the priests carried the ark into Canaan, the water came together, and the river ran again. The rocks were made into a monument to remember the crossing.

The Battle of Jericho

Joshua 5:10–6:27

After Joshua led the people of Israel into the promised land of Canaan, they celebrated Passover, because it was now springtime. The day after they arrived, they picked grain where it was growing, and made the flat Passover bread. And from that day on, the manna stopped falling. Instead the people ate what grew in their new country.

When Joshua came close to the city of Jericho, he suddenly saw a man with a sword standing in front of him.

"Are you for us or for our enemies?" Joshua asked.

"I am the captain of the Lord's army," said the man.

Joshua knelt down on the ground and bowed his head and worshiped. "What do you want me to do?" he asked.

The captain of the Lord's army said, "Take off your shoes. You are on holy ground." And Joshua did.

Now the gates of Jericho were shut tight, and all the houses inside the walls were locked, because the people had heard that Joshua and his army were coming.

God told Joshua, "I will give you the city of Jericho, even though it is a strong city. Here is what you must do. You and your men and seven priests blowing seven rams' horns will take the ark and march around outside the walls of the city once a day for six days. On the seventh day all of you must march around the city seven times, with the priests blowing their trumpets.

When they blow a seventh long blast on their trumpets, all of you will shout a great shout. Then the walls of Jericho will tumble down."

Joshua told his people what to do. "For the six days that we march, you must not make a sound. Don't even speak, until I tell you to shout."

Every day for six days, Joshua and his army marched once around the walls of the city, and then went back to their camp for the night. On the seventh day they marched around it seven times, with the priests blowing their trumpets. When the trumpets were blown for the seventh time, Joshua said, "Now shout! The Lord has given us this city."

The people shouted a great shout, and the walls of Jericho fell down.

Joshua Writes the Covenant

Joshua 23 and 24

Joshua was captain of the people of Israel. After Moses died, he took the people across the Jordan into the promised land. When he was a very old man, he told the elders of Israel, "I am old and ready to die." Then he called all the people of Israel to come together at a place called Shechem.

"This is what God says to tell you," he told the people. "God brought you out of slavery in Egypt and brought you across the Red Sea when Pharaoh's armies were chasing you. You lived in the desert a long time. Then God brought you across the Jordan River to this good land."

"Now," Joshua told them, "you must serve God faithfully. You must not worship the false gods that our grandparents worshiped in Egypt or the false gods of Canaan."

Joshua looked at the people. "As for me," he said, "and the people of my family, we will serve the Lord God."

"We will serve God, too!" the people answered. "God has taken care of us, and this is our God, too."

"Then throw away any idols of false gods that you have and obey the Lord."

They answered, "We will serve and obey the Lord our God, and no one else."

So Joshua made a covenant with God for the people. He wrote all the things down in the book of the law of God. Then he put a large stone up under an oak tree in the holy place of the Lord.

"This stone has heard all you said," Joshua shouted. "If you turn against the Lord your God, it will be a witness against you!"

Then Joshua sent the people to their own homes. When he was a hundred and ten years old, he died. The people buried him on his own land in the hill country at a place called Timnath-serah. And for many years after that, the people of Israel obeyed the Lord God.

The Story of Ruth

Ruth

Long before Jesus was born, a man named Elimelech, his wife Naomi, and their two sons lived in Bethlehem. There was a famine, and the family went to the land of Moab. There Elimelech died, and the two sons married two Moabite women named Orpah and Ruth.

Then the sons also died. Naomi decided to go home to Bethlehem. She kissed Orpah and Ruth and said, "Please go back to your own families and find other husbands. May God bless you!"

Orpah and Ruth wept. Orpah ruturned to her family, but Ruth pleaded, "Do not make me leave you. Wherever you go, I will go, and wherever you live, I will live. Your family will be my family, and your God will be my God."

So the two women went to Bethlehem. They arrived at the start of the barley harvest.

One day Ruth asked Naomi for permission to follow the harvesters and collect leftover grain in the fields. This is called gleaning. "I am sure someone will let me follow him," she said. Naomi agreed.

Ruth happened to go into the fields of Naomi's rich cousin Boaz. Boaz had heard how faithful Ruth was to Naomi. Now he saw how beautiful she was and how hard and humbly she worked. He welcomed her.

Soon Boaz arranged to marry Ruth. Ruth and Naomi were very happy. Boaz and Ruth had a son they named Obed. Obed's son was named Jesse, and when Jesse grew up, he had eight sons. One of them became King David.

Hannah and Samuel

1 Samuel 1; 2 Samuel 1–4, 11, 19–21

In the days when there were judges but no king in Israel, there was a man named Elkanah living in the hill country. In those days a man could have more than one wife. Elkanah had two. The first wife, Peninnah, had several children. The other wife, Hannah, wanted children but did not have any.

Every year this man and his family went to the city of Shiloh, to the temple that housed the ark of the covenant, to bring offerings to the Lord. And every year, when the family feasted after their offering, Hannah was too upset to eat. She felt sad to see Peninnah with all her children, and Peninnah would tease Hannah for not having children of her own. Even her husband, who loved her, could not make her feel happy.

One year after the feast, Hannah felt so sad that she went out near the door of the temple and cried and prayed that God would send her a child. She promised that if God would send her a baby, she would give the child to do God's work.

Eli the priest saw her crying and whispering. He asked her if she had drunk too much wine. "No, I am not drunk," Hannah said. "I have been praying to God about something that is making me very unhappy."

After Eli listened, he said, "Go in peace, and may the Lord answer your prayer." After they had talked, Hannah did not feel so sad.

God did not forget Hannah's prayer. The next year she had a baby boy and named him Samuel. When he was about two years old, she took him up to the temple for the first time, along with some food offerings.

Hannah walked up to Eli the priest and said, "Sir! O sir, I was the woman who was standing here praying and crying one day, and you saw me." She showed him her child, Samuel, and said, "I prayed for this child, and God has answered my prayer. So I am here to keep my promise. I have brought him to stay and serve God all his life."

Then they all bowed down and worshiped the Lord, and Hannah sang a song that began:

"My heart is joyful in God; God has made me strong!
I laugh at my enemies, because God has saved me.
There is no one as holy as our Lord, and there is no rock as strong as God.
The weapons of the strong are broken,
And the poor are given seats of honor."

Then Hannah and her husband went back to their home and left Samuel there to serve God.

Every year Hannah made a little robe for him. When her husband and the rest of the family went to Shiloh with offerings, Hannah took the robe up to the temple and gave it to her son.

Then Eli would say to Hannah's husband, "May God give you more children, because your wife has offered God her son Samuel."

And God was pleased with Hannah. She had three more sons and two daughters. Meanwhile Samuel grew up in the temple, serving God.

God Calls Samuel

1 Samuel 3:1–10, 19–20

Samuel's mother left him at the temple in Shiloh to live with Eli the priest and to serve the Lord. He was about two years old when she left him.

As Samuel grew older, Eli taught him all the things that had to be done to take care of God's temple. In those days God did not speak much to the people, and they did not have many dreams or visions of God.

While Samuel was still just a boy, he began to sleep near the place where the ark of the covenant was kept. Eli was getting old and could not see very well anymore. He slept in his own room.

One night while Samuel was asleep, God called, "Samuel! Samuel!"

The boy thought that Eli had called him, so he ran to Eli and said, "You called me. Here I am."

"I didn't call, my son," Eli said. "Go lie down."

After Samuel lay down, God called again. "Samuel! Samuel!"

Samuel got up and ran again to Eli. "Here I am. You called me."

"I didn't call, my son," Eli said. "Go lie down again."

Now Samuel did not know the Lord yet. God had not spoken to him before. So when God called Samuel a third time, he got up and went to Eli again. "You called me," he said. "Here I am."

Then Eli knew what was happening. He knew that God had called Samuel.

"Go lie down," Eli said. "And if God calls again, say, 'Speak, Lord, for your servant is listening.'"

So Samuel went back and lay down. Then God called, "Samuel! Samuel!"

"Speak, Lord, for your servant is listening," Samuel said. Then God told Samuel many things that were to happen in Israel.

Samuel grew up there at Shiloh. After that night God was with Samuel all the time and talked with him often. And soon all Israel, from north to south, knew that Samuel was a prophet of the Lord.

The Anointing of David

1 Samuel 8,15,16:1–13;
Augmented by verses from 1 Samuel 9 and 10

The people of Israel had lived for many years in the land God gave them. They had no king. Samuel, the prophet, was judge over Israel, and he made his sons judges, too. But they were not good men like Samuel. They took money from people, and they were proud and selfish.

The people began to cry out to Samuel, "You are old, and your sons are not good as you are. Who will guide us when you are gone? Give us a king, as other countries have!"

Samuel was unhappy when he heard these words. God spoke to him and said, "Samuel, listen to these people. It's not you they don't want. They have turned against me. They do not want me for their king. This is like all the other things that they have done, ever since I led them from Egypt."

Samuel listened as God went on. "Give the people what they want," God said. "But warn them that kings will do anything they want. Kings will take people's homes and food and animals. They will take children for slaves. When the people hate their king, they will cry out to me about him. But then I will not listen."

Samuel told the people, but they shut their ears. "We want a king, as other countries have," they shouted.

So God said, "Give them a king!"

God told Samuel to take perfumed oil and go to a tall, strong, handsome man named Saul. Samuel anointed Saul by pouring the oil over his head. Then he told Saul that God had called him to be the king over Israel.

But later Saul disobeyed God. And God told Samuel, "I am sorry I chose Saul." Samuel was angry and cried to the Lord all night. He thought his heart would break.

Finally God called to Samuel and said, "Stop thinking about Saul and making yourself unhappy. There will be a new king over my people. Go to a man named Jesse in the city of Bethlehem. One of his sons will be the next king."

So Samuel went to Bethlehem and found Jesse. They had a great feast, and Jesse called his sons together. One by one, they came to meet Samuel.

"This must be the one!" Samuel thought, as each fine, tall young man came.

But God said to Samuel each time, "I don't decide by how strong and handsome they are. I look at their hearts. This is not the one."

Seven of Jesse's sons came to Samuel, but God did not choose one yet. Samuel asked, "Do you have any other sons?"

"The youngest son is in the fields with our sheep," Jesse told him.

"Send for him at once," Samuel said, and someone went to bring the son home. When he came in, Samuel saw a handsome, healthy young man with sparkling eyes. The Lord said, "Samuel, this is the next king of Israel! Get up and anoint him with your oil."

So Samuel took his horn of oil and anointed the boy's head, in front of his father and brothers. From that day on, this young man was powerfully filled with God's Spirit. His name was David.

David and Goliath

1 Samuel 17:1–58

Saul was still king over the people of Israel when the Philistines started war with them. The Philistine army stood on a hill on one side of the valley, and the army of Israel stood on a hill on the other side.

Out of the Philistine camp came a giant of a soldier, named Goliath. He was about nine feet tall. He wore a great bronze helmet and armor and carried a huge spear made of heavy metal.

"Why haven't you come out to fight?" Goliath shouted across the valley at Saul's army. "Choose a man to fight me. If he can kill me, you win this war. But if I kill him, the people of Israel will be our slaves."

When Saul and the army of Israel heard these words, they were terrified.

Now the three eldest sons of Jesse were in Saul's army. The youngest of Jesse's eight sons was David, who took feed to the family's sheep at Bethlehem. One night Jesse told David, "Take this sack of grain and ten loaves of bread and ten cheeses to your brothers and their group in the army. Bring back news of how they are doing in the battle."

David got up early the next morning and left the sheep with a keeper. He set out with the food and got to the camp just as the army was getting ready to fight.

After David arrived, the giant Goliath came out on his mountain and shouted as before. When the men of Israel heard and saw him, they ran back, full of fear. The soldiers called to David, "Have you seen that giant who came to fight us? Anyone who can kill him will become rich and marry the king's daughter and not have to pay taxes."

David said, "Who is this Philistine giant? How does he dare come against God's own people?"

David's oldest brother heard him talking to the men and was angry.

"David, what are you doing here?" he cried. "Why have you left our sheep without anyone to watch them? You only came to see the fighting."

Soon the king heard about David and sent for him. David came to his tent. "Do not give up, sir," David said. "I will go fight the giant!"

"What?" cried Saul. "You are only a boy, and Goliath has been a soldier all his life."

But David told Saul, "I am my father's shepherd. If a bear or a lion tries to eat a lamb, I grab him by the fur and save the little one. I have killed both lions and bears, and I know how to kill this Philistine. God has saved me from the claws of lions and bears," said David. "God will save me from this giant who is against God's own people."

Saul cried, "Go, then! And the Lord go with you!" He gave David armor, a helmet, and a sword to wear. But when David put these heavy things on, he couldn't move, because he wasn't used to them. So he took them off.

David went to a little stream and picked five smooth stones. He put these in his shepherd's bag. He took his tall shepherd's stick and his leather sling and went to meet the giant.

Goliath came out and saw David. "Am I a dog? Do you come to chase me with a stick?" he roared at David. "Come up here, and I'll feed you to the birds of the air and the beasts of the field!"

David shouted back, "You come with a sword and a spear to fight. But I come in the name of the Lord of hosts, the God of the armies of Israel!"

The giant stood up and started toward the boy. David ran quickly toward the battle line. He took a stone from his bag and put it in his sling. Then he spun around and round and let the rock fly.

The stone hit Goliath in the forehead so hard that the giant fell on his face to the ground, dead.

When the Philistines saw that David had killed the giant without a sword or spear, they ran away. The army of Israel chased them for miles.

After Goliath was killed, Saul talked to David, asking him whose son he was. "I am David, Jesse's youngest son, and I come from Bethlehem." David answered.

David Brings the Ark to Jerusalem
2 Samuel 5–7

When he was thirty years old, David became king over Israel and needed a city to rule from. He fought the Jebusites and captured Jerusalem. He built a big house on Mount Zion, right in the middle of the city.

Later David and some other men went to bring the ark of the covenant up to Jerusalem. The ark was a special box with the ten commandments inside and was the sign of God's covenant with Israel.

When they came into Jerusalem with the ark, David felt such joy that he danced before the ark to worship the Lord. All the people shouted and sang. They held a great feast and gave offerings to God.

David was living in his house in Jerusalem, and one day he talked with Nathan the prophet.

"I live in a house made of fine cedar wood," David said. "But the ark of God only lives in a tent."

That night, God spoke to Nathan about the ark and about David. "All these years I have been worshiped in a tent. I have traveled where Israel has traveled. But now I want you to tell David that his son will become great. His son will build me a house for worship."

David was very surprised the next day when Nathan came to see him and said, "God has spoken to me and said, 'I took you out of the sheep pasture and made you king of Israel. I have been and will be with you. After you die, your son will be king. He will build a great temple for the Lord. And your kingdom will last forever.'"

David went into the tent of God and sat down to pray, "Who am I and who is my family to you? You have already done so much for us. Now you promise us even more. And I know your blessing will be on my family forever."

Solomon Builds God's Temple

1 Kings 5–8

King David and his wife Bathsheba had a son named Solomon who became king over all Israel and married the princess of Egypt.

Solomon remembered that God had said to his father, "Your son will build my temple in Jerusalem."

He sent a message to the king of Tyre, who had been a friend of his father's. "The Lord promised my father David that his son would build the temple. Now I want to begin. Please send your men to the hills of Lebanon to cut great cedar trees for me."

The king of Tyre was very pleased to get this message. He sent Solomon hundreds of cedars and pines by floating them in rafts down the Mediterranean Sea. Solomon also sent many men into the mountains to cut stone. Many more came to carve wood or to hammer the gold decorations.

The people of Israel began building the temple. They made it ninety feet long and thirty feet wide. It was forty-five feet high at the front, and about seventy feet high at the back.

The inside walls were covered with cedar, and the floor was pine. Solomon's workers made an inside room to be the most holy place, where the Ark of the covenant would stand. It had angels called cherubim carved in olive wood and covered with pure gold. All the walls in the temple had carvings of angels, palm trees, and flowers. All the floors were laid with gold.

A wonderful engineer named Hiram came from Tyre to help King

Solomon. He made two beautiful pillars with copper tops with lilies and pomegranates hammered into them. He made all the bowls and stands and bronze decorations.

Every thing to be used on the altar was made of purest gold, and even the hinges for the doors of the most holy place were gold.

It took Solomon and Hiram and thousands of workers of Israel more than seven years to build God's temple. When it was finished, Solomon had the ark of the covenant with the ten commandments in it brought from David's palace on Mount Zion. The elders and leaders and priests brought the ark into the new temple and set it in the most holy place.

When the ark was in its place, God's glory filled the temple in a great cloud.

King Solomon and all the people of Israel made offerings to the Lord. They feasted and sang and danced that day. When the people went home, they had joy in their hearts because of the goodness that God had shown to David and to Solomon and to all the people of Israel.

Elijah and the Widow's Bread

1 Kings 17:8–15;
Augmented by verses from 1 Kings 12, 14, 15, 16, and 18

When Solomon's son Rehoboam became king, the people of Israel went to war with each other. The country divided in two. The people of the north decided to call themselves Israel. The people of the south called themselves Judah.

There were many kings after that in both kingdoms. The kings often forgot the Lord God. One of the worst kings of Israel was named Ahab. He had a wicked wife named Jezebel, who talked Ahab into worshiping a false god named Baal.

At this time God spoke to a prophet named Elijah. This good man went to King Ahab, and tried to make him remember God's covenant. But Ahab would not listen. He built a temple and an altar to the false god and did more to make God angry than any other king that Israel had ever had.

Then Elijah said, "As the God of Israel lives, there will be no rain or dew in this land until I say so."

Then God told the prophet to go and hide himself in desert country east of the Jordan River. "You will drink from the brook Cherith, and the ravens will feed you," the Lord told Elijah. So Elijah did as God said. Ravens flew in with meat and bread for him every morning and every night, and he drank from the brook.

But after a while the brook dried up, because Elijah had commanded the sky to give no rain. Then the Lord told Elijah to go to a city called Zarephath.

"I have told a widow in that city to feed you," God told Elijah. So the prophet traveled to that city. When he came to the city gates, a widow was gathering sticks for a fire.

"Please bring me a drink of water," Elijah called to her. As she was going, he added, "Please bring me a piece of bread, too."

"I have no bread baked," the woman said. "And all I have in my whole house is a handful of flour and a few spoons of oil. I was gathering sticks for a fire, to make some bread for my son and me. Then after we eat it, we will die, because we have no more food. Nothing will grow without rain."

"Don't worry," Elijah said. "Make some bread for me and for yourselves. The God of Israel has told me that the flour will not be gone and the oil will not be used up until God sends rain back down to earth."

The woman went back to her house then and made Elijah a loaf of bread. And everyone in her family, as well as Elijah, ate for many days. They had all they wanted, and the flour and the oil were never used up before it rained again three years later.

Elijah and the Prophets of Baal

1 Kings 18:1, 17–45;
Augmented by verses from 1 Kings 17

When Ahab and Jezebel were king and queen of Israel, they began to worship the false god, Baal. The altars of the God of Israel were pushed over, and people forgot God.

Elijah was God's prophet. He told the king that God would take away all the rain and dew and nothing could grow. Then Elijah hid from King Ahab. He stayed with a widow and her family for many months.

After three years without rain, God told Elijah to go back and see King Ahab. When the king saw Elijah, he said, "Is that you, Elijah? Is that you, troublemaker of Israel?"

"I am not the one who has made trouble," said Elijah. "Dry land and hunger are here because you have forgotten the commandments and followed false gods."

Then he told Ahab to send the people to a mountain called Carmel. "Bring the four hundred prophets of the false god Baal. And have all those prophets who are such good friends with Queen Jezebel come, too."

So Ahab sent messengers out to the whole country, and the people and false prophets came.

Elijah stood up in front of everyone who was there. "You can't believe two things at once," he said. "How long will you sit on the fence? If our Lord is God, then follow the Lord. But if Baal is God, then follow Baal instead."

Then Elijah told them, "You will see the Lord's power. I am only one prophet for God. There are hundreds here for Baal. We will make an offering and see which God takes it."

So they laid wood on the altar of Baal. They killed a bull and put the meat on the altar. They did not light the wood but prayed instead.

From early morning until noon the prophets of Baal called him, "O Baal, hear and answer us!" But nothing happened.

At noon Elijah said, "Keep calling. Cry louder. If Baal is a god, Baal will hear you. Maybe Baal is on a trip, or busy, or taking a nap."

All afternoon the prophets of Baal raved on. Over and over, they called out, "O Baal, hear us!" But nothing happened.

Then Elijah called the people to him. He repaired the altar of God that had been torn down. He took twelve stones that stood for the twelve tribes of Israel and fixed the broken altar.

He dug a pit around the altar and put wood on top of it. He laid the meat of a bull on the wood and told people to pour buckets of water on it three times.

Then Elijah stood in front of the altar and cried out, "O Lord, God of Abraham and Isaac and Israel, show these people today that you are God! Answer me, Lord, so the people of Israel may know you and turn away from false gods."

Suddenly, God's fire fell from the sky, and burned up the offering. It burned up the wood, the stones, and the dust. It licked up the water in the pit.

When the people saw what had happened, they fell down. They hid their faces and worshiped, and said, "The Lord is God! The Lord is God!"

The prophets of Baal were taken away. Then Elijah told King Ahab to go back and eat and drink. While the king had dinner, Elijah went to the top of the mountain and knelt down and hid his face between his knees.

"Look toward the sea at the sky," he told his servant.

"I don't see anything," said the man.

Seven times Elijah said, "Go and look." Elijah stayed there on his knees, with his face in the dust. The seventh time the servant said, "I see a little cloud, as small as my hand."

"Go tell Ahab to go home in his chariot before it rains," said Elijah. But before Ahab could leave, the sky was black with clouds, the wind blew, and there was a great rain.

Elijah at the Mountain of God
1 Kings 19

God's prophet Elijah showed King Ahab and the people that the god Baal was false. Jezebel, King Ahab's wife, was filled with anger, because she was a believer in Baal. Jezebel sent a message to Elijah and swore that she would kill him.

Elijah felt tired and frightened. He got away quickly and went south to the desert of Judah. He sat down under a tree and asked God to let him die.

"I have lived long enough," he told the Lord. "Let me die." He lay down under the tree and slept. Suddenly an angel touched him and said, "Elijah, get up and eat."

Elijah looked around. Near his head was bread, baked on the hot stones, and a jar of water to drink. He ate and drank and slept again. Then the angel touched him a second time, and Elijah ate and drank again.

Then he had enough strength to walk to the very mountain where God gave Moses the ten commandments. It took him forty days.

He found a cave in the mountain and went in for the night. Suddenly God's word came to him.

"What are you doing here, Elijah?" God asked.

"O Lord," Elijah complained, "I have loved you for a long time, but your people have given you up. Your altars are torn down. Your prophets have been killed. Now I am the only one left, and they want to kill me, too."

God said, "Go out and stand before me, on the top of the mountain." So Elijah went out and God passed by.

First a great wind came. It was so powerful that it broke pieces of rock off the mountain. But the Lord God was not in the wind.

After the wind there was a great earthquake. But the Lord God was not in the earthquake.

After the earthquake there was a fire. But the Lord God was not in the fire.

But after the fire there came a still, small voice, like the sound of a gentle breeze. When Elijah heard the voice, he wrapped his face in his cape and stood at the entrance to the cave.

"What are you doing here, Elijah?" said the voice. Elijah answered again, "I have loved you for a long time but your people have given you up. Your altars are torn down. Your prophets have been killed. Now I am the only one left, and they want to kill me, too."

God told Elijah there were seven thousand faithful people left in Israel.

"Now go into Syria. Take oil and use it to anoint the man named Hazael to be king of Syria. Anoint the man named Jehu to be the king of Israel. Anoint the man named Elisha to be the next prophet."

The first person Elijah found was Elisha, plowing a field with oxen. Elijah came close and threw his prophet's cape over Elisha. Elisha said, "Let me say good-bye to my mother and father, and then I will come with you." He gave a feast for his parents and the farm workers. Then he followed Elijah to Syria.

Chariots of Fire

2 Kings 2:1–15

God was about to take Elijah, the prophet of Israel, up to heaven in a whirlwind.

Elijah and Elisha, his friend and follower, were walking to a town named Bethel. There was a group of men in Bethel called sons of prophets. These men came to Elisha and said, "Do you know that today God will take your master away?"

"Yes, I know," said Elisha. "Don't talk about it."

Then Elijah told Elisha, "Stay here. God has told me to go to Jericho." But Elisha would not leave him. In Jericho another group of prophets again told Elisha that Elijah would be taken away.

A second time Elijah told Elisha, "Please stay here. God has called me to come to the Jordan River." But again Elisha would not leave him, so they went to the Jordan together. Fifty sons of prophets followed them. They stood at a distance to watch what would happen.

Elijah took his cape, called a mantle, and rolled it up. Then he touched the water with it, and the river stopped so that Elijah and Elisha could walk across on dry land.

Then Elijah said, "If you have anything to ask from me, do it now."

"Let me have a double share of your spirit," said Elisha.

"This is a hard thing," Elijah told him. "Here is what you must remember. If you see me as I am being taken from you, you will have what you ask. If you don't see me, then you will not have it."

They walked and talked, and suddenly a chariot of fire appeared, pulled by horses of fire. Then Elijah was taken into heaven, and Elisha saw all of this.

"My father! My father!" shouted Elisha. "I see the chariots and horses of the God of Israel!" And then he could not see Elijah any more.

Elijah's mantle lay on the ground. Elisha picked up the mantle and hit the water in the river. He said, "Where is the God of Elijah?" Then the river parted, and Elisha walked to the other side.

When he got across, the sons of the prophets said, "The spirit of Elijah is now on Elisha." And Elisha was now the prophet of Israel.

Elisha Visits a Family

2 Kings 4:8–37

When the prophet Elijah was taken to heaven in the whirlwind, Elisha became God's prophet in Israel. He traveled through the land and showed God's power.

One day Elisha went to a town called Shunem. A very rich woman who lived there invited him to dinner. After this, Elisha often ate with this family when he was in Shunem. Soon the woman and her husband made a room on their rooftop for Elisha. They put a bed, a chair, a table, and a lamp in the room. Whenever Elisha was going through that part of the land, he stayed with these Shunammites in his own room.

One day, when he was visiting them, he wondered what could be done for the woman who had been so kind to him. Elisha's servant said, "She has no children, and she wants a son."

"This time next year, you will be carrying a baby boy in your arms," Elisha told the woman.

"Oh, that can't be! Please, as a man of God, don't tell me lies," said the woman. But what Elisha said was true. God gave her a son the next year.

And the child grew. One day he ran to his father in the fields.

"My head! My head!" he cried. His father had him taken inside, where he sat in his mother's lap for a few hours. Then he died. After laying him on Elisha's bed, the mother immediately got on a donkey and went to find Elisha.

Elisha was in his home on Mount Carmel when he looked up and saw the woman riding up. "It is the Shunammite woman," he said to his servant.

She came in, very upset. She could hardly talk. She took hold of Elisha's feet and said, "I didn't tell you to ask God for a son. I told you not to tell me lies!"

Elisha saw her pain and went at once to her house. He saw the little boy lying dead on the bed and went in and shut the door. First Elisha prayed to the Lord. Then he got up and lay down on top of the child. He put his mouth on the boy's mouth, his eyes on the boy's eyes, and his hands on the boy's hands.

As he lay there, the boy began to be warm again. Elisha got up and walked around for a moment. Then he stretched out on the child again. The boy sneezed seven times and then opened his eyes.

Elisha opened the door and told his servant to call the woman. "Come, pick up your little boy," he said when she came in. She looked and then bowed down to the floor in front of Elisha. Then she carried her little boy out, because he was well.

Naaman the Leper

2 Kings 5:1–15

Naaman was a famous man in Syria, the country north of Israel. He was captain of all the armies of the king of Syria. He was strong and brave, but he had a terrible skin disease called leprosy.

Now during a raid against Israel, Syria had captured some of the people as servants. One of them was a young girl who went to work for Naaman's wife. One day she said to the woman, "If only my master could go to the prophet of Israel. He would cure him of leprosy."

Naaman's wife told him what the young girl said. Then Naaman went to tell his king, who said, "You must go to Israel."

So Naaman brought a letter from the king of Syria to the king of Israel. It said, "I am sending Naaman to you to be cured of his leprosy."

The king of Israel cried, "What? Am I God? How can I cure a man of leprosy? The king of Syria is trying to pick a fight with me!" He got very upset and ripped his shirt down the front.

When Elisha the prophet heard about this, he sent a message that said, "Don't sit there tearing your clothes. Send the man to me. I will show him that God has a prophet in Israel."

So the king sent Naaman to Elisha's house. When the captain rode up with his chariot and horses, Elisha didn't go out. He sent a servant to say, "Elisha says for you to wash in the Jordan River seven times. Then you will be well. All the leprosy will disappear from your skin."

When Naaman heard this, he was very angry. "We have rivers in my own country!" he shouted. "If washing would take away leprosy, I could have gone to our own rivers." He started to leave, still angry.

But one of his own servants came up to him and said, "Sir, if the prophet told you to do something very difficult, you would do it. Then do this easy thing. Go down and wash in the river."

So Naaman went down to the Jordan River. He dipped himself in the river seven times. He did exactly what the prophet of God told him to do. Suddenly his skin was as soft and smooth as a baby's skin. He was well!

Then Naaman took all his servants and soldiers. He went back to Elisha and said, "I know now that there is no God anywhere on earth except the God of Israel!"

The Call of Isaiah

Isaiah 6:1–13

There was a war in Israel and the country was divided into two kingdoms. The northern kingdom was called Israel. The southern kingdom was called Judah. There was a man in Judah whose name was Isaiah, and God called him to be a prophet.

One day, while he was in the temple, Isaiah had a vision. He saw the Lord God seated on a high throne. God's robe filled the whole temple.

All around God were fiery angels called seraphim, each with six wings. One pair of wings covered their faces. One pair covered their feet. With the other two wings they flew, calling to each other, "Holy, holy, holy is the Lord God of Hosts! The whole earth is full of God's glory!"

When the seraphim called to each other, the temple shook like an earthquake. The whole room was filled with smoke.

Isaiah felt small and sinful when he looked at God and God's angels. He cried out, "There is no hope for me. I am a sinful man in a country of sinful people. Yet I have seen God with my own eyes!"

Then one of the seraphim flew to Isaiah. He was carrying a hot, glowing coal that he had taken from the altar with a pair of tongs. He touched Isaiah's lips with the hot coal.

Then the seraph said, "See, this has now touched your lips. You are not guilty now. Your sin is wiped away."

Then Isaiah heard God's voice. "Whom shall I send? Who will go for me?"

Isaiah answered, "Here I am. Send me."

"Go and tell the people," God said. "They may listen, but they will not understand."

"How long, O Lord?" asked Isaiah. "How long will it take for the people to understand?"

God said, "Until the cities are ruined and are left without people in them. The whole country will be empty and sad."

From that day Isaiah was a prophet of Judah. He told the people that they must listen to God or God would let their land be ruined.

The Desert Shall Bloom

Isaiah 35:1–10;
Augmented by verses from Isaiah 30–34

Isaiah was a prophet of Judah. He said that hard things would happen to the people in Israel and Judah because they disobeyed God. They worshiped false gods. They paid no attention to the people who were poor and hungry. They did what they wanted, without asking for God's help.

"The Lord is angry with you," Isaiah told them. "Your cities will fall down, and your farms will turn to desert."

Then Isaiah told the people something wonderful. "God says that after great unhappiness your teacher will come to you," he said. "He will make clear what you should do. And the Lord will heal you and make all the people strong and safe and happy."

Isaiah told them many beautiful things:

"The desert and the dry land will be glad again.
Flowers will bloom everywhere,
And the desert will sing.
The mountains and hills will see God's glory.

Help those who are weak and tired,
Tell those who are afraid not to fear;
God will come to save them.

The eyes of blind people will see,
And those who are deaf will hear again.
People who can't walk will run like deer,
Those who can't speak will sing for joy.

There will be water in the wild places
And streams in the desert.
The hot sand will become a lake,
And the thirsty ground will have springs of water.

There will be a great road through the desert.
It will be called the Holy Way,
And the people of God will walk there.
There will be no more sadness.
And the people will sing for joy."

The Lion and the Lamb

Isaiah 65:17–25

Isaiah was God's prophet. He told the people many terrible things that would happen if they did not change their ways and keep God's law.

But he told them good things, too. "Someday," said Isaiah, "God will make Israel new again!"

This is a song God gave Isaiah about Israel:

See! I will make a new heaven and a new earth,
All old things will be forgotten.
Be glad and rejoice forever in what I make.
See! I will make a happy Jerusalem,
And her people will be full of joy.
I will rejoice in Jerusalem
And be happy with my people.
No one will be unhappy.
Everyone will live to be a hundred.
They will build houses and live in them.
They will plant grape vines and eat their fruit.
I will hear them when they call to me.
The wolf and lamb will eat together,
The lion will eat hay like a cow.
They will not hurt or destroy
On all my holy mountain.

Jeremiah in the Well
Jeremiah 38:1–13

Jeremiah was a prophet of God in the city of Jerusalem. He said to the people, "God will let the army of Babylon destroy this city. Surrender to the Babylonians to save your lives. People who stay here will be killed or die of hunger and sickness."

Four princes of Jerusalem heard this. They went to King Zedekiah and said, "This Jeremiah is a troublemaker. The army and the people of the city will be weak and helpless if they listen to him. Let us kill him."

"Do what you wish," said the king.

So they took Jeremiah and threw him into a kind of deep well called a cistern. There was no water in it, but he stuck in the deep mud at the bottom.

Then Ebedmelech, an Ethiopian who worked at the palace, went to the king and said, "Sir, what those four princes have done to God's prophet was wrong! Jeremiah will die of hunger in there."

The king thought this over and told him, "Take some men from the palace and get Jeremiah out."

So he got three men, and they went to a storeroom and found old clothes and rags. They lowered the rags down into the cistern by ropes and called to the prophet, "Put these rags under your arms. Then the ropes won't tear your skin."

Jeremiah did what they said, and they lifted him safely out of the cistern.

The Babylonian Exile and Return

2 Chronicles 36:11–23;
Augmented by verses from Ezra 1, 2, and 7

The people of Jerusalem and the rest of Judah did more and more wicked things. Instead of worshiping God, they worshiped idols of false gods. Their kings were stubborn and did what was wrong in God's eyes. God sent many messengers and prophets, but they were ignored and laughed at.

Finally God was so angry at Judah that there was no escape. God let the armies of Nebuchadnezzar, the king of Babylon, come and destroy Jerusalem. They burned down the temple of God and smashed the walls of the city. The Babylonians even took all the fine gold bowls and other treasures out of the temple and carried them back to Babylon.

Many people were killed. Many were taken to Babylon as slaves. All the things that Jeremiah the prophet had told them came true. They stayed in Babylon for seventy years.

Then the Persian king, Cyrus, beat Babylon in a war. Cyrus told the Jewish people, "You may go back to your cities. Repair your walls and rebuild the temple." What Jeremiah had foretold came true. Cyrus returned all the gold treasures from the temple to the leaders of the tribes of Israel; and forty-two thousand three hundred and sixty people, plus their servants and singers and horses and camels, came back to the city of Jerusalem. They rebuilt the temple and kept the law that Moses had given them.

The Valley of Dry Bones
Ezekiel 37:1–14

The people of Judah disobeyed God over and over. God sent many prophets to them, but they did not listen. Finally their country was invaded by the Babylonians. Many people were captured and sent to Babylon.

In Babylon the people felt homesick and unhappy. Then God called Ezekiel to be one of their prophets in Babylon. He showed Ezekiel many wonderful things about heaven and earth.

One day Ezekiel had a vision. He saw the Lord leading him into a valley. As he looked around, he saw that the ground was covered with old, dry bones.

God said, "Tell these bones to come together and live, in my name."

So Ezekiel said, "Bones, hear the word of the Lord! God's breath will come into you and make you alive again. Then you will know that the Lord is your God."

Then in his vision Ezekiel heard the bones begin to rattle. They came together and made skeletons. Then he saw that the skeletons were covered with skin and muscle. They were people. But they still lay quietly, without breathing.

"God says that the four winds must come now and breathe God's breath on these dead people," cried Ezekiel. Then in his vision Ezekiel saw a great wind come and fill the bodies with God's breath. They came to life and stood up on their feet. There were enough of them to make a great army.

Then God explained the vision to Ezekiel. "The dry bones are the people of the house of Israel. They have been captured. They are far from the land I gave them. They feel as if their bones are dry, and they have no hope."

God told Ezekiel, "I will save this people once more. I will put my Spirit inside them, and they will truly live. Then all the people will go back to their own land, and I will be their God."

Daniel in the Lions' Den
Daniel 6

The people of Judah were captured by the armies of Babylon. One of the people captured was Daniel, who was a prince of Judah and God's prophet.

When King Darius of Persia conquered the kingdom of Babylon, he chose a hundred and twenty men to help him govern. Then he set three men up as presidents of the huge kingdom. One of these was Daniel.

The other officials became jealous because Daniel did better work. They planned a way to get rid of him. They convinced Darius to send out word to all his kingdom that nobody could pray to anyone except the king for thirty days. For that whole month nobody was supposed to pray to God.

Daniel learned about the order. Nevertheless every morning and every noon and every night he went to a room upstairs in his house. As usual, he got on his knees and bowed to God and prayed.

The jealous men spied on Daniel. Through an upstairs window they saw him praying. Then they rushed to Darius. "O king," they said, "didn't you say that anyone who broke this rule would be thrown into a pit full of lions?" The king agreed. "Well, we saw Daniel praying!"

The king was very upset. He loved Daniel, and he tried to find a way out of the rule. But the same men who spied came and said, "O king, you know that the Persian law can't be changed!"

So Darius called Daniel and told him he had to go into the lions' den. "Your God, whom you are so faithful to, will have to save you," he said. "You are a good man. I do not want you to be killed. But the law is the law."

Then at sunset the king had his soldiers throw Daniel into the lions' cave. A huge stone had been rolled in front of the door, so Daniel could not escape. Then the king went to his room, but he could not sleep.

At sunrise Darius ran to the lions' cave. As he got close, he cried, "O Daniel, God's servant! You who have never stopped serving your God! Has God been able to save you from the lions?"

Daniel called, "Live forever, O good king Darius! God shut the lions' mouths so they could not hurt me. God knew I had done no wrong to God or to you."

Darius was full of joy. He had Daniel taken out of the lions' den, and the soldiers who pulled him out saw that he didn't have even a scratch.

Then the king sent a message to every city in his kingdom, saying, "In my kingdom people should fear and respect the Lord God whom Daniel worships. God's kingdom will last forever! God does miracles and saves people. God has saved Daniel from lions."

The Story of Jonah

Jonah

God told a prophet named Jonah, "Go to the great city of Nineveh, and tell the people there that their wickedness will be punished."

Jonah didn't want to go to Nineveh. He thought he could run away from God, so he got on a ship that was sailing to Tarshish. Jonah didn't want to go to Nineveh because he hated the people of Nineveh and did not want to warn them of God's wrath.

But God saw what Jonah did and sent a terrible storm. The sailors and passengers threw dice to see whose fault the storm was. The dice said it was Jonah's fault.

"Who are you? And why has this storm come?" the people asked.

"I am a Hebrew. I worship the God of heaven who made the sea and the land," Jonah told them.

By now the sea was becoming so stormy that they thought the ship might sink.

Jonah told them that he was running away from the Lord.

"What are we to do?" they cried.

"Throw me into the sea," said Jonah. So they threw him off the ship into the waves of the ocean. Then the storm stopped, and the sailors saw the power of God and praised God.

The Lord called a great fish to swallow Jonah. He was in the belly of the fish for three days and three nights.

From inside the fish Jonah prayed and thanked God that he had not drowned. God spoke to the fish, and the fish spit him out on the beach.

Then Jonah obeyed God and went to Nineveh and preached to the people. "In forty days the Lord will destroy this city because of your wickedness!" he shouted.

The people believed him. They put on ragged clothes to show how sorry they were, and they began to pray and go without food. Even the king put on ragged clothes, went without food, and said, "Let us all in this city pray to God and be sorry for our sins! Maybe this will change God's mind."

God did see that the people had changed and were no longer wicked, so God did not destroy their city.

Jonah was angry at God. "You made me come here and warn these people that they would be destroyed," he told God. "But I knew this would happen. You have been merciful and changed your mind about punishing them. Well, just kill me then, because I don't want to live."

God said, "Jonah, what right do you have to be angry at me?"

Then God made a plant grow up where Jonah sat outside the city. Jonah was thankful to God because the plant made shade for him. But the next morning God sent a caterpillar to ruin the plant, and the plant wilted and died. When the sun came up, it was so hot that Jonah almost fainted.

"Let me die!" Jonah shouted at God. "I would rather die than live."

"What right do you have to be angry with me, Jonah?" asked God. "You feel sorry for this plant, and you didn't even make it grow yourself. Why can't you understand that I feel sorry for my people in Nineveh?"

CHRISTIAN SCRIPTURE

The Birth of John the Baptist

Luke 1:5–25, 57–76

In the days when Herod was king of Judah, a priest named Zechariah lived in Jerusalem. He and his wife Elizabeth were getting old and still had no children.

One day, as Zechariah was burning incense in God's temple, he had a vision of an angel. (A vision is a kind of a dream from God.) He saw the angel come and stand by the altar.

Zechariah was frightened. But the angel said, "Zechariah, don't be afraid. God has heard your prayers, and your wife Elizabeth will have a child. You will name him John, and he will grow up to be God's prophet."

Zechariah said, "My wife and I are very old. How can I be sure this will happen?"

"I am Gabriel, the angel who stands near God. I was sent to tell you this news. Since you did not believe God's message, you won't be able to speak again until the child is born."

Zechariah came out of the temple, unable to speak. All the people who were there knew he had had some kind of vision.

Months later Elizabeth's baby was born. Her neighbors were full of joy because God had heard her prayers for a baby. "His name is John," said Elizabeth.

But everyone said, "He should be named Zechariah, like his father."

Zechariah remembered what Gabriel said. He still could not speak, so he wrote on a tablet, "The child's name is John."

As soon as he wrote that, Zechariah was able to speak again. Then all their friends and neighbors knew that this baby was special to the Lord God.

Zechariah was full of God's Holy Spirit. He sang a wonderful song that said, "Blessed be the Lord God of Israel! God has saved us and will bring a savior from the house of David. You, child, will make the people ready for the Lord's coming."

The Annunciation to Mary

Luke 1:26–38, 46–47

The angel Gabriel went to a city in Nazareth where a young woman named Mary lived. Mary was planning to be married to a man named Joseph. Joseph was from the family of the children and grandchildren and great-grandchildren of King David.

"Hail, favored one!" cried Gabriel, when he saw Mary. "The Lord is with you!"

Mary was surprised and afraid. But Gabriel said, "Do not be afraid, Mary. God is pleased with you. You will have a son, and you will call him Jesus. He will be a king forever."

"How can this be?" asked Mary. "I do not have a husband."

The angel told her, "God will send the Holy Spirit to you. Your child will be God's son!"

Mary said, "I am God's servant. Let what you have said happen."

Not long after, Mary decided to visit her cousin Elizabeth. She went to the hill country of Judea to the house of Zechariah and Elizabeth.

Elizabeth was going to have a baby soon. When Elizabeth heard Mary's greeting, the baby moved inside her. Elizabeth was filled with the Holy Spirit and said, "You are the most blessed of women and blessed is the child you will have!"

Then Mary sang a song about God:
"My soul sings of the greatness of
the Lord.
My spirit rejoices in God my Savior!"

The Birth of Jesus

Luke 2:1–20

When Caesar Augustus was emperor of Rome, he sent an order to all the empire that everyone should report for a census. In Judah, where Herod was king, each man went to the city where he was born and reported for his family.

A man from Nazareth, whose name was Joseph, went to report to Bethlehem because he was from the family of David. With him was Mary, his wife, who was expecting her baby very soon.

While they were still in Bethlehem, the time came for Mary's baby to be born. There was no room for them to stay at the inn, so she had her baby in a stable where animals were kept. She wrapped him in cloths and laid him in a manger, a box full of soft hay. She named the baby Jesus.

Nearby, there were shepherds who stayed overnight in the fields to protect their sheep. They were sitting outside under the stars, when suddenly an angel of the Lord appeared to them, and the glory of the Lord was shining all around them.

"Don't be afraid!" called the angel. "I bring you wonderful news of great joy. A savior, who is Christ the Lord, has been born to you today in David's city of Bethlehem. Here is how you will know him. You will find a baby wrapped in swaddling cloths and sleeping in a manger."

Suddenly the whole sky was full of angels, praising God and saying,

"Glory to God in the highest,
And peace to God's people on earth!"

When the angels had gone, the shepherds said to each other, "Let's go to Bethlehem, and see this wonderful thing that God has told us!" And they rushed to Bethlehem and found Mary and Joseph and the baby Jesus, who was sleeping in a manger.

When the shepherds saw the baby Jesus, they told Mary and Joseph what the angels had said. Mary thought about these words for a long time.

The shepherds went back to their fields, singing and talking about God's glory.

The Coming of the Wise Men
Matthew 2:1–12

After Jesus was born in Bethlehem in the days when Herod was king, some wise men came to Jerusalem from a country far away.

"Where is the child who is the new king of Israel?" they asked. "We saw his star. We have come to worship him."

King Herod, who was cruel and wicked, heard about these wise men. He asked all the priests and the teachers of the law, "Where will the messiah be born?"

They said, "The prophets have told us that he will come from Bethlehem."

So Herod secretly sent for the wise men. "Go to Bethlehem," he said. "Search all around. When you find the child, come back and tell me, so that I can go worship him, too."

And so the wise men left for Bethlehem. Suddenly they saw the star again and were very joyful. They followed the star until it came to rest over the place where Jesus was. They went in and found the baby Jesus with his mother Mary. They bowed low and worshiped him. They brought him presents of gold and frankincense and myrrh.

God told the wise men in a dream not to go back to the king. So, instead of returning to King Herod to tell him about the baby, they went home another way.

The Presentation of the Baby Jesus in the Temple

Luke 2:22–39

When Jesus was a month old, his parents took him to the temple in Jerusalem, to be presented to God. They brought a sacrifice of two pigeons as thanks for their son. They did this to keep the law of Israel.

There was an old man in Jerusalem named Simeon who was wise and good. The Holy Spirit had told Simeon that he would see God's Christ, or Messiah, before he died.

On the day that Mary and Joseph brought Jesus to the temple, Simeon met them inside. He took the baby in his arms, blessed God, and said,

"Lord, you have set your servant free
To go in peace as you have promised.
My eyes have seen the Savior,
Whom you have given for all people.
A light for all the nations
And the glory of your people Israel."

There was also at the temple a woman prophet named Anna. She was eighty-four years old and spent every day at the temple, praying and worshiping. She was coming into the temple just when Mary and Joseph were there.

She gave thanks to God and talked about Jesus to everyone who was waiting for Jerusalem's freedom.

After Mary and Joseph had done everything according to the law of Israel, they left Jerusalem and went to their home.

The Escape to Egypt

Matthew 2:13–23

When Mary and Joseph were still in Bethlehem and Jesus was a baby, an angel came to Joseph in a dream.

"Get up quickly," said the angel. "Pack your things and take Mary and the baby Jesus to Egypt. Stay there until I tell you to leave, because King Herod has plans to look for the child and wants to kill him. Herod thinks this baby will take away his throne!"

So Joseph got up in the middle of the night. He took the baby and his mother, and they left for Egypt right away.

They stayed in Egypt until King Herod died. Then God's angel came again to Joseph in a dream. "Get up and go back to the land of Israel. The one who wanted to kill Jesus is dead now," the angel told Joseph. So Mary and Joseph took Jesus back to their own country. They went to live in the town of Nazareth in Galilee.

The Boy Jesus in the Temple

Luke 2:41–52

Mary and Joseph and Jesus walked from Nazareth to Jerusalem every year for the feast of Passover. The journey was almost a hundred miles, and it took several days. Mary, Joseph, and Jesus went with friends, and camped at night.

When Jesus was twelve, he and his family went to Jerusalem as usual. Jesus stayed in the city after they left, but his family didn't know that. They thought he was with relatives or friends. That evening Mary and Joseph went from camp to camp, looking for him. They couldn't find him. The next day they checked with all their friends and relatives. Nobody knew where Jesus was.

After three days of looking, they went back to the temple in Jerusalem. There was Jesus, listening to the teachers of Scripture and asking them questions. Everyone who heard him was surprised, because Jesus understood so much about God.

When Mary and Joseph found him, they ran to him. "Son, why have you done this to us?" cried his mother. "Your father and I have been searching the countryside for you for three days. We were sick with worry!"

Jesus said, "Why were you worried? Didn't you know I would be doing my Father's work, in His house?"

Mary and Joseph were not sure what Jesus meant. But then he went with them and obeyed them all the time after that. He grew taller, and he grew wiser, and he pleased both God and people. But Mary thought for many years about his words in the temple.

John the Baptist Preaches

Matthew 3:1–12

John was the son of Elizabeth and Zechariah the priest. He was born to them when they were old, and he was a cousin of Jesus.

When John grew up, he went to live in the wild desert country. When he camped near the Jordan River, people came in huge crowds to hear his words because they knew he was a man of God.

"Repent! Turn away from doing wrong," John told them. "Stop being wicked and be good, because God's kingdom is near!"

When people heard John speaking, they remembered that Isaiah the prophet had said hundreds of years before that there would be "A voice, calling out in the wilderness, 'Make a straight road for the Lord.' "

John wore rough clothes made from camel's hair and a leather belt. All he ate was locusts and wild honey. When the people from Jerusalem and all Judea came out to hear him, they told the truth about their sins and asked to be forgiven. Then John baptized them in the Jordan River.

Now many of the temple teachers and fine people from Jerusalem also came to be baptized. They were called Pharisees and Sadducees, and many of them were rich and proud and selfish.

"You nest of snakes!" John shouted at the Pharisees and Sadducees. "Who said you could get away from the punishment to come? Show that you are truly sorry. It isn't enough just to be in the family of Abraham. If God wanted to, God could make children of Abraham out of these rocks!"

John told the people that he baptized them with water but that someone else was coming soon. "He is much greater than I am," said John. "I am not good enough even to carry his sandals. He will baptize you with the Holy Spirit and with fire."

Jesus Is Baptized

Matthew 3:13–17

Jesus left his home in the part of Israel called Galilee. He went to the Jordan River and asked to be baptized by John the Baptist.

"How can this be?" asked John. "It would be better if you baptized me!"

Jesus said, "Let it be this way for now, so everything will be right."

Then John took Jesus to the water and baptized him. As soon as he was baptized, Jesus came out of the river. Suddenly the skies were opened, and he saw God's Spirit coming down on him like a dove. He heard a voice from heaven say, "This is my beloved Son, with whom I am well pleased!"

The Temptation of Jesus
Luke 4:1–15

When Jesus was baptized in the Jordan River, he was filled with the Holy Spirit. Then the Spirit led him out into the wild desert country, or wilderness. There he was tempted by the devil for forty days.

Jesus ate nothing during that time, and he was hungry. The devil said, "If you are the Son of God, turn these stones into bread."

Jesus answered the devil by saying, "Scripture says that people must not live just by bread."

Then the devil took him up high, where they could look down on all the great kingdoms of the world.

"All of this is mine," said the devil. "I will give you all of these kingdoms, if you will worship me."

But Jesus said, "Scripture says, Worship only God, and serve nobody but God."

So the devil took Jesus to Jerusalem and set him on the highest tower of the temple.

"If you are really God's son, throw yourself off this tower," he told Jesus. "Scripture says that God will send angels to guard you."

Jesus answered, "Scripture also tells us not to tempt the Lord your God!"

After he had tempted Jesus in every way, the devil left. Then Jesus, filled with the power of the Spirit, returned to Galilee. People began to tell each other about him, and they went to the places where he taught.

Jesus Teaches in the Synagogue
Luke 4:14–30

One sabbath day Jesus went to the synagogue in his home town, Nazareth. This was a place where the Scriptures were taught.

In the synagogue Jesus read from the book of the prophet Isaiah:

The Spirit of the Lord is upon me,
because God has anointed me
to tell good news to poor people,
to let prisoners free,
to make blind people see,
and to call this the Lord's year.

After he read these words, Jesus closed the book and sat down. Everyone was watching him. Jesus said, "These words have come true, right here in this room."

Everyone was surprised at the way he spoke. "Isn't this Joseph's son?" they asked.

And Jesus said, "You want me to do a miracle! Prophets can be welcomed everywhere except in their own town."

This made them very angry. So they grabbed him and took him up to a cliff. They were going to throw him off, but he managed to get away.

Fishing for People

Luke 5:1–11

Jesus was walking by a large lake called the Sea of Galilee. People crowded all around Jesus to hear him talk.

Jesus saw two boats pulled up on the beach. One of them belonged to Simon Peter. Jesus climbed into it and asked Simon Peter to take the boat out on the lake a little way. Then more people could see and hear Jesus.

When Jesus finished talking, he said to Peter, "Sail out into the deeper water. Then put out your nets to catch fish."

Peter cried, "What? Master, we have fished all night, and we didn't catch a thing! But if you say so, I will try." So he put his nets into the water. When he pulled them in, there were so many fish in them that the nets were breaking, and he had to call his partners to help him.

Peter sank to his knees in front of Jesus. "I am not good enough to be with you," he said.

"Don't be afraid," Jesus said. "From now on, you will not catch fish. You will be fishing for people, and catch them for God."

Peter and his partners, James and John, left home and followed Jesus.

The Beatitudes:
Jesus Talks about Blessings

Matthew 5:1–12

Everywhere that Jesus and his disciples went, crowds followed. One day, when Jesus saw how many people wanted to hear him, he and his disciples went up on a hillside and sat down. Then he began to speak:

"Blessed are the people who know they need God," Jesus told them. "The kingdom of heaven belongs to them.

"Blessed are the people who are sad. God will comfort them.

"Blessed are the gentle people. Someday God will make the whole earth theirs.

"Blessed are the people who feel hungry and thirsty for fairness and goodness. God will give them all they hope for.

"Blessed are the people who are kind to others. God will be kind to them.

"Blessed are the people with pure hearts. They will see God.

"Blessed are the people who make peace. They will be called God's children."

Finally he said, "Blessed are those who are treated badly when they love God and do God's work. God will give them the kingdom of heaven."

A Wedding at Cana

John 2:1–12

One day Jesus went to a wedding in Cana, a small town near the Sea of Galilee. His mother, Mary, and some of his new friends and disciples went with him.

In those days a wedding party lasted for several days. Everyone came to celebrate, and the groom had to buy plenty of food and wine.

There was not enough wine at this wedding, and Mary felt sorry for the bride and groom. She whispered to Jesus, "They are running out of wine! Please, do something."

Jesus said to her, "What has that got to do with me? My time hasn't come yet."

But his mother went to the servants who served the dinner and said, "Do whatever he tells you."

Jesus went over to the servants and said, "Fill these jars with water." These were big twenty-gallon jars filled with water for Jewish rites of cleansing.

The servants filled the big jars to the rim. Then Jesus told them, "Now take a cup full to the steward who is in charge of this feast."

The steward tasted what they brought him. Then he turned to the bride and groom.

"Most people serve the best wine first and then give the people cheap wine later. But you have saved the very best wine for last!"

This was the first miracle that Jesus did. His disciples believed in him.

After the wedding Jesus and his disciples went to Capernaum, a town on the lake, and stayed there for a few days with his mother and his brothers.

Lilies of the Field

Matthew 6:19–34

Jesus did not want people to worry about earning enough money or having fine clothes or owning beautiful things.

"Don't collect treasures here on earth," he said. "Robbers can break into the house and steal your money or your things. Moths can eat holes in your fine clothes. Rust can ruin things. Instead, collect treasures in heaven. Nothing can spoil them there. You see, your heart will be where your treasure is!"

Some people who listened to Jesus worried about having enough food to eat or clothes to wear. He reminded them that the birds don't plant seeds or cut grain, but that their Creator feeds them.

"Think about the wild lilies in the field," he said. "They don't work. They don't sew clothes. But they are more beautiful to look at than King Solomon in his finest robes! If God takes care of the flowers and birds, don't you think God will take care of you, too?"

"Your God knows what you need," Jesus said. "Start thinking about God's kingdom first. Then everything you really need will come to you."

A House Built on Rock

Matthew 7:24–29

This is a story that Jesus told.

Two men built new houses. One was a very wise man. His house was strong and safe because he built it on rock.

The other man built a house, too. But he was foolish and built it on a very sandy place.

Now a terrible storm came. Hard rains poured down on the two new houses. Winds blew and broke the treetops.

The house that was built on rock stood through the whole storm. The rain and wind and flood couldn't hurt it.

But the foolish man who built his house on sand was not happy. When rain and wind and flood came, the water washed away the sand, and his house crashed down!

Jesus said, "The people who hear my words and do what I say are like the man who built the house on rock. No matter what happens, their faith makes them strong."

Then he said sadly, "But there are other people who hear my words and pay no attention. They do whatever they want. When things get hard for them, they are not strong, because they do not have a strong faith."

People were surprised at this story. "This man knows what he is talking about," they said.

Jesus Asks Matthew to Follow Him

Matthew 9:9–13

One day Jesus saw a man named Matthew sitting in his office. Matthew was a tax collector. He worked for the Roman government.

"Matthew, come with me and be my disciple." Jesus said. Matthew got up right then and went with Jesus.

Nice people did not usually eat dinner with tax collectors, because most of these tax collectors cheated the people. But Jesus ate dinner with Matthew and other tax collectors and others who were rejected by the people.

When the Pharisees saw this, they asked the disciples, "Why does your teacher eat with tax collectors and sinners?"

Jesus heard them and said, "People who are healthy don't need doctors. I came to help people who need my help."

The Twelve Disciples

Matthew 9:35–10:8

Jesus was going from town to town, teaching about God, telling the good news, and healing people. When he saw such huge crowds, he felt sorry for them, because they were like sheep without a shepherd to take care of them.

He told his disciples, "The harvest is ready, but there are not enough people to cut the grain. Pray that God will send workers!"

So he called his twelve disciples and gave them his power over evil spirits and sickness. The names of these twelve were Simon Peter and his brother Andrew; James and John, the sons of Zebedee; Philip and Bartholomew; Thomas and Matthew the tax collector; James, the son of Alpheus, and Thaddaeus; Simon the Zealot and Judas Iscariot, the one who betrayed Jesus.

Jesus sent them out to the towns in Galilee and Judea. He said, "Tell the good news to the lost people of Israel. When you go, say, 'The kingdom of heaven is here!' Heal the sick, raise the dead, and cast out evil spirits. Don't take any money for what you do, because God gave you these gifts without making you pay for them."

A Man Who Could Not Walk

Mark 2:1–12

One day, when people heard that Jesus was at home in Capernaum, they crowded into his house. Everyone wanted to hear what he said. Everyone wanted to see him and touch him. The house and porch and yard were filled with people.

Four men came carrying their friend on a stretcher. He wasn't able to walk, and they wanted Jesus to heal him. But they couldn't even get to the front door.

"I know," said one. "Let's try getting in through the roof." So they took the stretcher with their friend on it up on top of the house. They pulled tiles off the roof until there was a big hole over the place where Jesus was standing. Then they put ropes on the stretcher and lowered their friend down into the room.

Jesus saw that these people had real faith. So he said to the sick man, "Your sins are forgiven."

Some teachers of the law were shocked. "Only God can forgive sins!" they said.

Jesus said, "I will prove that I can forgive sins." He turned to the crippled man and said, "Get up, pick up that stretcher, and walk!"

The man stood, picked up the stretcher, and went out where everyone in the crowd could see him. The were all surprised and joyful. They praised God, saying, "We have never seen anything like this in our lives!"

Picking Grain on the Sabbath
Mark 2:23–28

Jesus and his disciples traveled around the country near the Sea of Galilee, teaching about God and healing sick people. One sabbath day (when the Jewish people rest and worship God), Jesus and his friends were walking through a field. On the way his friends picked some grain to eat.

"What?" said some Pharisees, who thought they were better than most people. "Your friends are picking grain on the sabbath. That is against our Jewish law. No work should be done on the sabbath day."

Jesus replied, "Didn't you ever read in Scripture that once King David and his army ate the holy bread in the tabernacle? It was all right because they were so hungry, even though no one was supposed to eat that bread except priests. God made the sabbath for people. God didn't make people for the sabbath! The Son of man is lord even over the sabbath."

The Mustard Seed

Mark 4:30–34

This is a story Jesus told.

The mustard seed is very small. When it falls to the ground, we can hardly see it. But then what happens?

The seed hides in the dark ground. The sun warms it. The rain makes it swell and burst open. Then shoots come forth and make a plant.

When the plant grows up, it is like a small tree! The tiny seed has become a bush that puts out branches where all the birds of the sky can come and rest and make nests.

"This is what the kingdom of God is like," Jesus told his friends.

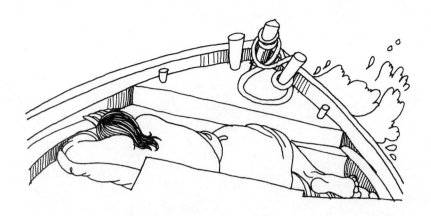

Jesus Calms the Storm

Mark 4:35–41

One day Jesus stood in Peter's boat and taught crowds of people who were on the lake shore. They stayed until evening. Then Jesus said to his disciples, "Let's cross to the other side."

They began to cross the Sea of Galilee. Jesus curled up on a cushion in the back of Peter's boat. He didn't wake up when a storm came.

Soon there were hard rains and terrible winds. The sailboat was tossing in the great waves and filling up with water. Jesus' friends woke him up and said, "Teacher, wake up! We're going to drown! Don't you care?"

Jesus stood up and said to the wind and waves, "Peace! Be still!"

At that very moment the storm stopped, and the Sea of Galilee was very calm.

Jesus turned to his disciples. "Why are you so frightened?" he asked. "Don't you believe that God will take care of you?"

The disciples were too surprised to answer. They said to each other, "Who is this Jesus? Even the wind and the sea obey him!"

The Lame Man at the Pool

John 5:1–15

Jesus went to Jerusalem for a feast. Now in Jerusalem near the sheep gate there is a pool called Bethesda, with five porches around it. On these porches lay sick and blind people and people whose arms or legs could not move.

The sick people were waiting there for the water to move. An angel from God went down every now and then and made the water bubble and move. Then anyone who stepped in the water right after that would be healed.

One man was there who had been ill for thirty-eight years. Jesus knew that he had been lying there for a long time, and he went to talk to him.

"Do you want to be healed?" Jesus asked him.

"Sir," said the man, "The trouble is that I don't have anyone to put me in the pool. So when the water is stirred up, other people get there while I am trying to climb down the steps."

Jesus said, "Get up, and pick up your mat, and walk." And the man picked up the things he was lying on and walked away, healed.

Now it was the sabbath day, when the people of Israel are supposed to rest. So some said to the man who was healed, "Why are you carrying that mat on the sabbath?"

"The man who healed me said to pick up my mat and walk," he told them.

"Who was he?" they asked. But the man didn't know who Jesus was. And by now Jesus was out of sight.

Later Jesus found him in the temple. "You are well now," said Jesus. "Do not sin. Something worse could happen to you!"

The man went away then and told the people who talked to him that it was Jesus who had healed him.

Can the Blind Lead the Blind?

Luke 6:39–49

These are some sayings that Jesus told the people who came to him.

Can a blind person lead another blind person someplace? Won't they both fall in a ditch? A student isn't better than the teacher.

How is it that you can see the tiniest speck in your friend's eye, but you don't notice the log in your own eye? First take the log out of your own eye and then look at your friend's speck.

A good tree doesn't have bad fruit on it. A bad tree doesn't have good fruit. Every tree can be known by its fruit. You can't get figs from a thorn tree. And you can't pick grapes off a bramble bush.

Why do you call me "Lord, Lord," if you don't do what I say? If a person comes to me and does what I say, that person is like a good carpenter. He carefully builds a strong house. When the storm comes, it will not fall down.

The Centurion's Servant
Luke 7:1–10

There was a centurion in Capernaum who needed Jesus. (A centurion was a Roman army officer in charge of a hundred soldiers.) This centurion had a servant who was a friend to him. The servant was very sick and close to dying. The centurion had heard about Jesus and sent some Jewish leaders to ask him to come and make his servant well.

The leaders came to Jesus and said, "This Roman is a good man. He loves our country. He even built the synagogue where we study and worship!"

So Jesus started to go with them to the man's house. But before they arrived, the centurion's friends came running out with a message.

The message from the centurion said, "Lord, I am not good enough for you to come into my house. That is why I didn't come for you myself. But I understand giving orders. When I say to a man, 'Come,' he comes. If I say, 'Go,' he goes. If I say I want something done, it is done. It is the same with you. Just say the word, and my servant will be healed. I know this."

Jesus was surprised. "Nowhere in all Israel have I seen such faith, not even among God's own people!"

The friends went back to the centurion's house and discovered that his servant was well.

Feeding Five Thousand People

John 6:1–14

Jesus went up into the hills of Galilee with his disciples. A great crowd followed him because they had seen him heal those who were sick.

It was almost time for the Passover festival. Jesus looked at the crowd of people. He turned to his disciple Philip. "How are we going to get enough bread for them all to eat?" he asked. He really asked this just to see what Philip would say.

"It would cost many dollars to buy even a tiny piece of bread for each of these people," Philip answered.

Then Andrew, another one of the disciples, said, "There is a boy here who brought five small barley loaves and two fishes. But what good will that do, when there are so many people?"

Jesus said, "Ask the people to sit down."

Everyone sat down on the grass. There were at least five thousand people.

Jesus took the bread and thanked God for it. He gave it to the people. Then he did the same with the fish. All the people had as much as they wanted to eat.

Then Jesus said to his disciples, "Gather up all the crumbs and small pieces, so we don't waste any." They went around and picked up all the leftover pieces, and there was so much left that it filled twelve baskets.

When the people saw all this, they cried out, "This has to be the prophet that God promised us!"

Jesus and the Little Girl

Luke 8:40–42, 49–56

One day a man named Jairus rushed up to Jesus. He fell at his feet and begged Jesus to come to his house and heal his sick daughter. This man was president of the synagogue, where people came to worship God and study the Scriptures. His daughter was about twelve years old.

While Jesus and Jairus were on their way to see her, a servant ran up and said, "It's too late. The little girl is dead. Don't bother the Teacher any more."

But Jesus said to Jairus, "Don't be afraid! Only believe, and she will be well." And he kept walking.

When they got to the house, Jesus allowed only Peter, James, and John and the girl's parents to come inside. Everyone was crying.

"Don't cry. She is only asleep," said Jesus. Some of the people laughed because they knew she was dead.

Then Jesus went to the bed where she lay. He took her hand and said, "Child, arise!" At once her spirit came back into her, and she stood up.

Jesus took her to her parents. "Give her some food now," he said. They were astonished, but Jesus said, "Don't tell anyone about this!"

The Man Who Was Born Blind

John 9:1–40

One day when he was out walking, Jesus saw a blind beggar. The beggar had been blind all his life.

"Why is this man blind, Teacher?" asked his friends. "Did he do something wrong? Or were his parents bad, so that God punished them?"

"No," said Jesus. "He did nothing wrong, and neither did his mother and father. But the world will now see the power of God."

He took some dirt and spit on it. He mixed it into clay and put this on the man's eyes.

"Now go and wash in the pool they call Siloam," he told the man. So the man went and washed. When he came back, he could see!

The neighbors and others who had seen him begging by the road side said, "Isn't this the blind beggar? He isn't blind now!"

"Yes!" said some people. But others said, "It's just someone who looks like him."

Then the man himself said, "Yes, I was the blind beggar."

"What happened?" everyone asked.

"A man named Jesus came. He put clay on my eyes and told me to wash in the pool," he said. "I don't know where he is now."

The man was taken to the Pharisees. "We know this Jesus," said some Pharisees, who thought they kept the law of Israel better than anyone else.

"We are sure that he is not from God. It is against the law to do this on the sabbath."

"But if he isn't from God, how can he do such things?" someone called out.

"What do you think of him?" someone else asked the man who was healed.

"He is a prophet," said the man.

Then some people said that the whole thing was a lie. "He wasn't ever really blind," they said. But they asked the man's parents, who told them he had been born blind.

"We don't know how any of this can be," the parents said. "We only know that once he was blind, but now he can see. Ask him yourself. He can talk."

The Pharisees said to the man, "If you are healed, thank God. Don't thank Jesus. He is a sinner."

They argued for hours, and the man kept saying, "All I know is this. I was born blind. Now I can see!"

"We follow the law of Moses," the Pharisees said. "We don't know anything about where this Jesus comes from."

"What?" said the man. "You don't even know where he comes from, but he walked up and made me see. You know that God doesn't listen to sinners but hears the prayers of people who do his will. Never in all time has there been a man who could heal someone born blind. Jesus is from God, or he couldn't do this."

"How dare you try to teach us?" cried the Pharisees. They made the man leave the synagogue.

Jesus heard about all this, and he went to see the man. "Do you believe in the Son of man?" he asked.

"Who is he, sir?"

"He is speaking to you and you are looking at him," answered Jesus.

"Lord, I believe!" said the man, and he worshiped Jesus.

"There is more than one way to be blind," said Jesus. "I came into the world to help those who can't see."

The Sower

Matthew 13:1–9, 18–23

Here is a story that Jesus told.

A farmer went out to sow seeds. As he threw the seeds, some of them fell along the path. Hungry birds came and ate them up.

Some other seeds fell where the ground was rocky. These started to grow right away. But they could not get enough water because their roots were not deep. Soon the hot sun made them wilt and die.

Thorny weeds grew where some of the seeds fell. The seeds started to grow, but the weeds grew faster. They choked the new plants, and they died.

But some of the seeds fell on the good ground. These grew, and got tall, and gave grain. Some gave thirty or sixty grains on a stalk. Some gave a hundred grains.

Here is what this story means.

When someone hears God's word about the kingdom of heaven but doesn't understand, the devil comes and grabs it away. This is like the seeds that fell on the path and were eaten by birds.

Some people hear God's word and are joyful. But when troubles come, they give up. This is like the seeds that fell on rocky ground and didn't have good roots.

Some people hear God's word, but they can't give up worrying about money and other things. So they never live God's way. This is like the seeds that fell into the thorny weeds.

But people who hear God's word and understand it are like the seeds that fell on good ground. These grew thirty or sixty or even a hundred grains on each stalk.

The Wheat and the Weeds

Matthew 13:24–30, 36–43

This is a story that Jesus told.

A farmer planted wheat seeds in his fields. One night, while he and his helpers were sleeping, an enemy secretly came and planted some weeds in the fields, too.

When the plants came up, the weeds came up, too. The farmer's helpers came and said, "Sir, didn't you plant good wheat seed in your fields? Well, there are weeds growing in them, too."

The man went and looked out over his farm. "An enemy has done this," he said.

"Do you want us to go out and pull the weeds?" asked his helpers.

"Oh, no!" he said. "You might step on the small wheat plants, or accidentally pull them up with the weeds. Let them grow together until the harvest. Then we can separate them."

When the wheat was tall and yellow and ripe, the farmer said, "Now we will harvest." They picked all the weeds first, tied them in bundles, and threw them into the fire. Then they cut all the wheat and stored it in the farmer's barn.

When Jesus told this story, he said, "This is the way it will be in God's kingdom. The angels will come and get all the wicked people and throw them out of the kingdom. But those who follow God's ways will shine like the sun in the kingdom of their Creator. If you have ears, listen to this."

Jesus Sends Seventy-Two People To Teach

Luke 10:1–12, 16–20

One day Jesus sent seventy-two of his followers to tell people the good news about the kingdom of God. They were to go in pairs to towns that he planned to visit later.

"The world is like a field of grain," he explained. "There is a big crop of people to teach, but not many workers to take in the harvest.

"I am sending you to dangerous places," he warned them. "But I want you to go peacefully. Don't take any extra clothes or food or money. Instead, when you come to a town, pick out people of peace and stay at their houses. Eat what the people give you. Don't move from house to house."

Before they left, Jesus said, "When you get into a town, tell everyone that the kingdom of God is close to them. Heal all the sick. But if the people won't listen and they are rude to you, leave the town."

When the seventy-two disciples came back, they were very joyful. They told about the healings that they could do in the name of Jesus.

"God's enemy is beaten now," Jesus told them. "And you should be very happy, because your names are written in heaven."

The Good Samaritan

Luke 10:25–37

One day when Jesus was talking to people, one of the lawyers from the temple asked, "Teacher, what must I do to receive eternal life?"

Jesus answered, "What does the law of Israel say about that?"

The lawyer said, "The law says that we must love God with all our hearts, and with all our strength, and with all our souls, and with all our minds. And we must love our neighbors as ourselves."

"Good!" said Jesus. "You have answered right. Keep this law and you will live."

"But who is my neighbor?" the man asked.

Jesus said, "I will tell you a story. Once a man left Jerusalem and started down the road to Jericho. Some robbers came, took all his money and clothes and his donkey, and beat him up. They left him half dead by the side of the road.

"A priest from the temple came down the road, saw him, and went to the other side of the road so he wouldn't have to look at him. A Levite (a temple helper) did the same thing. But then along came a Samaritan."

The people looked at each other. They wondered what Jesus was telling them. None of them thought the Samaritans were very good people.

Jesus continued, "The Samaritan saw the man and his heart went out to him. He put medicine and bandages on him, lifted the man onto his donkey, and took him to an inn.

"The Samaritan paid the innkeeper with his own money and asked him to take care of the man who had been robbed until he got well. He even promised to pay anything extra the next time he came to the inn."

Jesus looked at the lawyer. "Which one of the people was a good neighbor to the man? The priest? The Levite? Or the Samaritan?"

"The one who helped him," said the lawyer.

"Good," said Jesus. "Now go and do the same yourself."

Mary and Martha

Luke 10:38–42

Near Jerusalem is a village named Bethany. Jesus often stopped there to visit Mary and Martha, two sisters who were his friends.

One day when Jesus came there, Martha invited him in. Then Martha rushed around, fixing dinner and making the house neat.

Her sister Mary wanted to listen to what Jesus said. So she sat at his feet, looking up at him and listening.

But Martha still had a lot to do. She came and said to Jesus, "Lord, don't you care that I have to make dinner and clean up all by myself? Tell my sister to come and help me!"

Jesus said, "Martha, Martha! You are worried and upset about too many things. Mary has chosen well by sitting here and listening to me. It will not be taken away from her."

The Good Shepherd
John 10:1–16

In Israel, where Jesus lived, there were many sheep. In those days people did not put up fences to keep their sheep safe. Instead, they sent a shepherd to take care of them.

On cool nights the shepherds put the sheep into a pen, or sheepfold. On warm nights shepherds slept outside with their sheep and watched for robbers or wolves. A good shepherd would take care of the sheep even if he had to do something dangerous.

Jesus told his friends, "The shepherd enters the sheepfold by the door. He calls his sheep by name and they know his voice and follow him. They don't follow strangers."

"I am the good shepherd," said Jesus. "My sheep know my voice and come only to me. I am like the door to the sheepfold. You may come into God's kingdom by me."

"I would die to save my sheep," Jesus told them. "I have sheep in other flocks, but I will bring all the flocks together. There shall be one flock and one shepherd."

The Lord's Prayer
Luke 11:1–4; Matthew 6:7–15

The disciples saw Jesus praying. When he was finished, one of them asked, "Lord, teach us to pray."

Jesus said, "You don't need many words to pray. Your Father in heaven knows what you need."

This is the prayer that Jesus taught his friends:

Our Father, who art in heaven,
hallowed by thy name,
thy kingdom come,
thy will be done,
on earth as it is in heaven.
Give us this day our daily bread.
And forgive us our trespasses,
as we forgive those
who trespass against us.
And lead us not into temptation,
but deliver us from evil.

Some of the words in the prayer may be hard to understand. Here is another way to say the same prayer:

Our Father in heaven,
hallowed be your name,
your kingdom come,
your will be done,
on earth as in heaven.
Give us today our daily bread.
Forgive us our sins
as we forgive those
who sin against us.
Save us from the time of trial,
and deliver us from evil.

When Jesus taught his friends to say this prayer, he reminded them to forgive others. "Forgive people for what they do to you," he said. "Then your Father in heaven can forgive your sins, too. If you don't forgive, God can't forgive you, either."

Jesus Walks on Water

Matthew 14:22–33

Jesus spent a long day on the shore of the Sea of Galilee. He taught people about God and healed the sick. In the afternoon, he told the disciples to start without him. So they got into their boat and started across the lake.

Jesus sent the people to their homes. Then he went up into the hills by himself to pray. He was there when it began to get dark.

The disciples were still on the lake. The wind was blowing against them and pushing the boat backward.

In the middle of the night they saw Jesus, walking on the water toward the boat. They were terribly frightened and cried, "It's a ghost!"

"It's not a ghost," said Jesus. "Be brave. It's Jesus. Don't be afraid!"

Peter called out, "Jesus, if it's really you, tell me to walk to you on the water."

And Jesus said, "Come."

Peter got out of the boat and started toward Jesus. But as soon as he felt the wind, he got frightened and began to sink into the sea.

"Help me!" Peter cried.

Jesus took him by the hand right away and said, "Why did you stop trusting me?"

As they got back into the boat, the wind stopped blowing. And the disciples in the boat said to Jesus, "Truly you are the Son of God."

Invited to a Feast

Luke 14:1, 7–14

Jesus was invited to a dinner party. The people who came to the party were Pharisees and lawyers. They thought they kept the law of Israel better than anyone else. Jesus told them these things:

"When you are invited to a dinner party, don't shove into the front seats where important people sit. You will feel terrible if the host comes and says, 'You'll have to move and make room for someone important.'

"Instead, sit in the worst seat of all. Then the host will say, 'My friend, come up to a better place!' In the kingdom of God people who make themselves important will be made humble. People who are humble will be made important.

"When you give a party, don't just invite friends or relatives or rich people. Those people will invite you to their houses to pay you back. Instead, invite some people who are poor or blind or ugly or lame. They can't pay you back, but on the day of the resurrection, God will pay you back for being generous to them."

The Lost Sheep

Luke 15:3–7

This is a story Jesus told.

There was a man who had a hundred sheep. They were all fine sheep, and he took good care of them. One night, when he counted them, he noticed that one of the sheep was missing.

He searched and searched for his lost sheep. Finally he found it, laid the sheep on his shoulders, and came home, singing with happiness. When he got home, he said to all his neighbors, "Be glad with me! I have found my sheep that was lost!"

Jesus said, "It's the same in heaven. There is more joy in heaven over one person who decides to follow God, than over ninety-nine people who have been good all their lives."

The Prodigal Son

Luke 15:11–32

This is a story that Jesus told.

Once there was a rich man who had two sons. The younger one said, "Father, give me my share of your property now."

So the man gave him his share. A few days later the younger son took all his things and went to a far country. While he was there, he used up all his money enjoying himself.

When all his riches were gone, the young man was hungry and poor. He went to a man who gave him a job feeding pigs. He was so hungry that he would have eaten the pigs' food.

Suddenly he came to himself. He thought, "My father's servants have more than enough to eat. Why should I stay here and die of hunger? I will go to my father and say, 'Father, I have sinned against God and done wrong to you. I am not good enough to be called your son anymore. Let me work as one of your servants.'"

So the young man started off to his father's house. While the son was still a distance away, his father saw him coming. He ran out to meet his son and hugged and kissed him.

"Father," said the son, "I have sinned against God and done wrong to you. I am not good enough to be called your son."

But his father paid no attention to what he said. He called to the servants, "Bring the best clothes, and put them on my son, and put a ring on his hand and shoes on his feet. And kill the fat calf for a feast! My son was dead, and now he is alive again!" So they all had a happy party.

The older son came in from working in the fields and heard the music and dancing.

"What's going on here?" he asked a servant.

"Your brother has come home, and your father has killed the fat calf for a feast of celebration."

The older brother was angry and wouldn't go inside. His father came out and begged him to come in, but he replied, "Look, Father, all these years I've stayed here and worked with you like a slave. Did you ever give even a small party for me and my friends? But when this son of yours shows up after wasting so much money, you kill the fat calf and have a big feast!"

His father said, "Son, you are always with me, and everything I own is yours. But we have to be glad and celebrate today, because your brother was dead and is now alive. Once he was lost, but now he is found!"

Jesus Heals a Deaf Man

Mark 7:31–37

Jesus and his friends went to a part of the country called Decapolis, or Ten Towns. Many people came to see him and brought sick people to him.

One day someone brought a man who was deaf. He could not hear. He also could not speak clearly.

Jesus took him away from the crowd. He put his fingers into the man's ears and touched the man's tongue. Then Jesus looked up to heaven and sighed. "Be opened!" he said.

The man's ears began to hear. He was able to talk so that people could understand.

"Don't tell anyone about this," Jesus told the man and his friends. But the more he told them to be quiet about his miracles, the more they told everyone. People began to say, "Jesus can do everything! He can even make deaf people hear and speak!"

Peter Is Given His Name

Matthew 16:13–20

One day Jesus asked his disciples, "Who do people say that I am?"

They told him, "Some say you are John the Baptist. Some say Elijah, or one of the other prophets, come back to life."

"But who do you say that I am?" he asked.

Simon Peter said, "You are the Christ, the Messiah, the Son of the living God."

Jesus said, "You are blessed, Simon, son of Jonah. Nobody on earth told you these things. God in heaven told you. And from this day on I will call you Peter, which means 'the rock.' On this rock I will build my church, and not even death will be able to defeat that church. Peter, I will give you the keys to the kingdom of heaven. Whatever you forbid on earth will be forbidden in heaven. Whatever you allow on earth will be allowed in heaven."

Then he told them, "Don't tell anyone else at all that I am the Christ."

The Wicked Servant

Matthew 18:23–35

This is a story that Jesus told.

Once a king decided to find out how much his servants owed him. He wanted to make them pay. He looked over the bills, and he discovered that one of his servants owed him ten thousand silver coins!

"You must pay me now!" said the king.

"Sir, I cannot pay now!" said the servant.

"All right, then," said the king, "I will sell you as a slave. I will sell your wife and children as slaves. That will pay me what you owe."

The servant was so upset that he fell on his knees and began to beg the king, "Please, sir, do not sell us! Be patient. I promise I will pay you as soon as I can."

The servant cried and begged so hard that the king felt sorry for him. He said, "Very well. I will not sell you. I will forget that you owe me anything. You may go free."

The servant was full of joy. He left the king's palace. As he was walking down the street, he saw a friend who was another one of the king's servants.

Now this man owed the first one less than a silver coin. The first one grabbed him and said, "Pay me what you owe me!"

"I can't pay right now. Please be patient. I will pay you as soon as I can," said the friend.

"No!" said the first servant. So he had the man put in jail because he could not pay.

Some of the people who worked at the palace saw what happened. They were very upset, so they told the king. The king sent for his servant.

"You wicked servant!" said the king. "I planned to forget about your bill of ten thousand coins, but you put a man in jail for less than one coin. I was kind to you, and you should have been kind to the other man. Now you will go to jail until all of your bill is paid to me!"

When Jesus told this story, he said, "This story is about the kingdom of God. If you don't forgive others, God can't forgive you. You must truly forgive in your hearts."

The Workers in the Vineyard

Matthew 20:1–16

Jesus told this story to his disciples.

Once there was a man who grew grapes in a vineyard, or grape field. There was much work to do in the vineyard. So early one morning the owner went to the town to hire some workers. He said to some men, "I will pay you one piece of silver for the day."

"That's fine," they said, and went to work.

About three hours later he saw some other men, standing around outside. He told them, "If you go work in my fields today, I will pay you what is right."

At noon he hired more men. At three o'clock in the afternoon he hired some more workers.

Finally, at five that evening, there was only one more hour to work. The owner saw some men standing around the town.

"Why aren't you working?" he asked.

"Nobody gave us a job today," they said.

"Go to my fields and work," he said. So they went and worked for an hour.

At the end of the day he gave a silver piece to each of the men who went to work for only an hour. He also gave a silver piece to the ones who went to work at three o'clock and at noon and at nine. Finally, he paid each of the first men who went to work a silver piece.

Then some of the workers said, "We worked all day for a piece of silver. They worked only an hour, but you paid them the same thing! Is this fair?"

The man who owned the vineyard said, "My friends, I haven't hurt you. You said you would work for a piece of silver, and that is what I paid you. I can pay people what I want when it is my own money, can't I? Are you angry because I was kind to the last few men?"

Jesus Heals Ten Men

Luke 17:11–19

Jesus and his disciples went to Jerusalem. On the way they met ten lepers. These were men with a terrible skin disease called leprosy. Lepers were not allowed to come near other people. Everyone was afraid of catching the disease. Lepers could not live in regular houses or eat with other people.

The ten lepers stood back from the road. They called out, "Jesus, Master, have mercy on us!"

Jesus looked at them and said, "Go to the temple and show your skin to the priests." They started off, as he told them. While they were going, the leprosy was healed.

One of them looked at his skin and began to praise God with a loud voice. He ran back to Jesus, fell down on the ground in front of him, and kissed his feet. This healed leper was from the country of Samaria.

Jesus said, "Weren't ten men healed? Where are the other nine? Didn't anyone else come back and praise God and give thanks? Is this man from another country the only one?"

Then he said, "Stand up and go. Your faith has made you well!"

Two Sons

Matthew 21:28–31

This is a story Jesus told.

There was a man who had two sons. One day he said to one of his sons, "My son, go and work in the grape fields."

"No," said the first son. "I don't want to work in the fields today."

But later he thought about his father. He was sorry for saying no to him. So he went out and started working in the grape fields.

The father went to the other son and said, "Son, go and work in my grape fields today."

"Certainly," he said. "I'm on my way right now."

But he never got there. He went somewhere else and did what he wanted.

When Jesus told this story, he asked his friends, "Which one of the sons did what his father wanted?"

"The first one, who said he didn't want to go," they answered.

"That is what God's kingdom is like," said Jesus.

Invitations to a Wedding

Matthew 22:1–10; Luke 14:15–24

This is a story that Jesus told about the kingdom of heaven.

Once there was a king whose son was getting married. The king decided to give his son a huge wedding supper. He bought fine food and decorations. Then he invited all his friends.

But his friends did not come.

So the king sent his servants out to remind them. "Tell them I have cooked a great dinner and it is all ready," he ordered them.

But the friends did not come.

One sent a message saying, "I have just bought a new farm, and I am busy with that."

"I have some business in the city," said another.

Everyone sent excuses. Some of them were cruel to the king's servants who brought the invitations. Some servants even got killed.

Then the king was very angry. He sent his army to find the wicked men who killed his servants. The army burned down their farms.

"The ones I invited were not worth my invitation," the king said. "So go out into the streets and invite everyone you can find to the palace for a feast."

So the servants went out and invited everyone they saw, bad and good, and the palace was full of guests.

The Poor Woman and the Judge

Luke 18:1–8

Jesus told this story to his friends.

Once there was a judge who was not honest. He was not afraid of God. He was not afraid of people. He did anything he wanted.

There was a poor woman who lived in that city. She wanted the judge to do something about her enemy. She said the enemy had been unfair to her.

Morning, noon, and night the widow followed the judge around crying, "Make my enemy do what is right!"

"No," said the judge, every time.

But soon things got worse. It seemed to him that the woman was everywhere, bothering him all the time.

"I can't stand any more," said the judge to himself. "I am not afraid of God. I am not afraid of people. But if I don't help her, she will drive me crazy." So he made the woman's enemy do what was right.

After Jesus told this story, he said, "This judge was a wicked man, but a poor woman could make him do what was right, because she never stopped asking. Your God in heaven is a good judge. If you keep asking for God's help, God will answer."

Jesus Talks about the Law of Israel

Matthew 22:34–40; Mark 12:28–34

Jesus was in the temple in Jerusalem, and some Pharisees came to him. Now the Pharisees believed that they kept the law of Israel better than anyone else. They did no work on the sabbath day. They said all the right prayers. They washed their hands in special ways before they ate. They were very proud, and they were always looking for ways to trick Jesus.

One of the Pharisees stepped up to Jesus and asked, "Teacher, in all the law of Israel, which commandment is the greatest one?"

Jesus answered, "The Lord our God is the only God. Love the Lord your God with all your heart, and with all your soul, and with all your mind, and with all your strength. This is the first and greatest commandment. The second one is like it. It says that you shall love your neighbor as much as you love yourself. Everything the prophets say and the whole law are really about these two commandments."

The Pharisee and the Tax Collector
Luke 18:9–14

One day Jesus told a story about people who thought they were better than others.

Two men went to the temple to pray. One was a Pharisee, and one was a tax collector.

(Now Pharisees were very proud. They thought that they kept the Law of Israel better than anyone else. Tax collectors usually didn't have many friends, because they worked for the Roman army. They often cheated people out of money.)

When the Pharisee prayed, he stood up and said, "O God, I thank you that I am not like other people. I am not a cheater or unfair. I do not look at other men's wives. I give a tenth of my money to the temple. I go without food on certain days to be holy. I thank you that I am not like that tax collector praying over there."

But when the tax collector prayed, he didn't even look at heaven. He looked at the floor and struck himself on the chest. And all he said was, "God, be kind to me, because I am a sinner."

After he had told the story, Jesus said, "The tax collector went home in the right with God, and the Pharisee did not. To be great in God's kingdom, people must be humble on earth."

Zacchaeus in the Sycamore Tree

Luke 19:1–10

When Jesus visited the town of Jericho, a rich man named Zacchaeus wanted to see him. Now Zacchaeus was a very rich tax collector who worked for the Roman army.

The day Jesus came, Zacchaeus tried to get through the crowd to peek at him, but the crowd was too thick. He tried to see over the tops of their heads, but he was too short.

Then he thought, "I know! I'll climb that tall sycamore tree down the road. Then when Jesus comes by, I'll be able to see him."

So he ran on ahead of the crowds and climbed up the tree. When Jesus got there, he looked up at Zacchaeus in the tree.

"Zacchaeus," called Jesus. "Hurry up and come down. I want to go to your house today."

Zacchaeus scrambled down the tree and took Jesus to his home. He was filled with happiness.

"Look at that Jesus!" grumbled some people. "He is eating with a tax collector who cheats people!"

But Zacchaeus stood up at his table and said, "Lord, I want to give half of everything I own to the poor, right now. And if I have cheated anyone, I will give back four times as much as I took."

Jesus said to him, "Today God's love is in this house, and Zacchaeus is saved."

The Transfiguration of Jesus

Mark 9:2–13; Matthew 17:1–9; Luke 9:28–36

One day Jesus took Peter, James, and John and went up on a high mountain where they were alone. While they were there, Jesus was suddenly changed.

His clothes were shining whiter than anyone could wash them. Then the disciples saw Jesus talking with Moses and Elijah, two prophets who had lived hundreds of years before.

Peter could hardly think. He said, "Teacher, it is good that we are all here! Let's make three little houses from tree branches. One for you, one for Moses, and one for Elijah."

All three of the disciples were frightened and confused, seeing Jesus so changed.

Suddenly a cloud came over them, and a voice in the cloud said, "This is my Son, the one I love. Listen to him!"

Then the three men fell to the ground and covered their faces. When they looked up, Moses and Elijah were gone, and Jesus looked just as he always had.

On the way down the mountain, Jesus said, "Do not tell anyone yet about what you saw up there."

Jesus and His Friend Lazarus

John 11:1–44

Jesus got a message from his friends Mary and Martha.

"Our brother Lazarus is very sick. We know you love him. Will you please come?" said the message.

Now Jesus loved Mary and Martha and Lazarus. But instead of going to Bethany, where they lived, he stayed where he was for two days. Then he said to his disciples, "Let's go to Bethany."

The disciples said, "Jesus, should we go there? Not long ago the people in that region tried to kill you."

But Jesus started out, and they followed. As they were going, Jesus said, "Our good friend Lazarus is asleep. I will wake him up."

The disciples didn't understand that Lazarus was really dead. So they said, "If he is asleep, he will get well, won't he?"

"Lazarus is dead," Jesus told them. "What will happen next will help you to believe in me."

His friends could certainly not understand what he meant. When they got to the edge of town, they heard that Lazarus had been dead four days.

When Martha heard that Jesus was coming, she ran out to meet him. But her sister Mary sat in the house.

"Lord, if you had been here, Lazarus would be alive!" Martha cried when she saw Jesus. "I know that even now God will give you anything you ask for."

"Martha, your brother Lazarus will rise from the dead," said Jesus.

"Yes, I know that sometime, at the last day, he will rise again," she said. "That will be at the resurrection."

Jesus said, "I am the resurrection! I am the life! Whoever believes in me will have a new life. Do you believe this, Martha?"

Martha looked at Jesus. "Yes, Lord," she said. "I believe that you are the Christ, the Son of God."

Then she went to her house. "Come, Mary," she whispered to her sister. "Jesus is here, and he is asking for you."

Jesus was still at the edge of town. When the people of Bethany saw Mary get up quickly and leave the house, they followed her. They thought she was going to the tomb to cry for Lazarus, and they wanted to comfort her.

She ran to where Jesus was talking to his friends. She knelt at his feet crying and said, "Lord, if you had been here, my brother wouldn't have died."

When Jesus saw how unhappy she was and how many people who came with her were also crying for Lazarus, he was terribly sad.

"Where is Lazarus lying?" he asked.

"Lord, come with us and see the tomb," they said. Jesus cried, too.

When people saw Jesus crying with Mary and Martha, they said, "See how he loved his friend!"

But some others said, "He made a blind man see. Why couldn't he help Lazarus?"

By this time they were at the tomb, which was in a cave. Jesus was very, very sad, but he told the people to take the stone away from the door.

Martha said, "He has been in there for four days, dead! Why open the tomb now?"

Jesus said, "Didn't I tell you that you would see God's wonderful work, if only you believed?"

So some strong men rolled the stone away from the door of the tomb. Then Jesus looked up at heaven and said, "Father, I thank you for hearing me!"

Then he looked at the tomb. In a loud voice he cried, "Lazarus! Come out!"

And Lazarus came out. He was no longer dead. Jesus had made him live again.

The Blind Beggar

Mark 10:46–52; Matthew 20:29–34; Luke 18:35–43

Jesus and his disciples visited the town of Jericho. When they left Jericho to go to Jerusalem, many people followed them.

A blind man named Bartimaeus was sitting by the roadside begging. When he heard that Jesus was walking down the road, he began to shout. "Jesus, Son of David, have mercy on me!" he cried. Many people tried to hush him, but the more they tried, the louder he shouted, "Jesus, Son of David, have mercy on me!"

Now when Jesus heard the man's cry, he stopped and said, "Ask that man to come here."

The people called to Bartimaeus. "You're lucky. Jesus is calling you. Get up and go to him."

Bartimaeus threw off his cape and jumped up. He went to where Jesus was standing.

"What do you want?" asked Jesus.

"Teacher, I want to see again," said the blind man.

"Go in peace," said Jesus. "Your faith has healed you." And with that, Bartimaeus could see. And after that, he followed Jesus to Jerusalem, giving glory to God.

The Widow's Penny

Mark 12:41—44

Jesus went up to Jerusalem for the Passover feast. He walked around the city, teaching and healing. One day he sat down near the temple treasury, where people dropped their money offerings for God. Some very rich people put in many dollars.

Finally, a poor old woman came along. Her husband had died. She wore ragged clothes and did not have much to eat. She put in two coins. Together they were worth one penny. It was all she had.

Jesus told his friends, "This poor woman gave more than all those rich people. They have so much money that they will not miss what they gave. But this woman gave all the money she had in the whole world."

Being Ready for God

Mark 13:26–27, 35–37

When Jesus taught the people about God, he warned them that they should always be ready for God.

"Someday you will see the Son of man returning in the clouds with power and glory. God will send angels to every nook and cranny on earth and bring together the people God has chosen.

Then Jesus said, "So stay awake and pray! You won't know when the moment will come. God is like a man who goes on a trip and tells all his servants to do their work while he's gone. He expects the doorkeeper at the door to stay awake! Nobody knows when the owner of the house might return. It could be at dinnertime or in the middle of the night or very early in the morning."

Ten Women with Their Lamps

Matthew 25:1–13

This is a story that Jesus told about the kingdom of heaven.

There were ten young women who were bridesmaids. It was their job to keep their oil lamps bright, so they could light the way for the bridegroom when he came. Then they would all go to the wedding feast together.

Five of these young women were very wise. They took extra oil for their lamps. But five of them were foolish. They did not take oil to the place where they waited.

Now the bridegroom was very late, and the women all fell asleep. Suddenly they heard someone cry out, "The bridegroom is coming!"

The wise bridesmaids filled their lamps with oil and the lamps glowed brightly. But the foolish women had no light, because they were out of oil.

"Give us some of your oil!" they cried to the others.

"But then there won't be enough for all of us," said the wise bridesmaids. "Run to the store and buy some."

While the foolish women were trying to buy oil, the bridegroom arrived with a great crowd of friends. The five wise young women held up their lamps, and walked in front of the bridegroom to light his way to the house. Then they all went in and locked the door.

Soon the foolish women got back. They pounded on the door and cried, "Let us in!"

But the bridegroom shouted through the door, "I don't open my door to strangers in the middle of the night!"

When Jesus told this story, he said, "This is the way some people are with God. Be ready when God calls!"

A Story about Money

Matthew 25:14–30

This is a story that Jesus told.

A man called all his servants together and said, "I am going on a trip. I will give you each some money to take care of for me."

Then he gave each one as much money as he thought that each of them could take care of. To the first one he gave five gold coins, called talents. To the second he gave two gold coins. To the third he gave one gold coin.

Then he went away for a long time. When he came back, he called his servants. "How have you taken care of my money?" he asked.

The first one said, "Master, I took the five gold talents and used them to earn five more." Then he gave to his master ten coins.

"Well done!" said the man. "You are a good and faithful servant. A person who can be faithful with a little bit will be put in charge of more." And he made the servant one of his managers.

The second one said, "Master, I took the two gold talents you left with me and used them to earn two more."

"Well done!" said the man. "You are a good and faithful servant, too." And he made that servant one of his managers.

Then the third servant came and said, "Master, I know you are a very careful man. You try to get every cent you can out of anything you do. So I was afraid. I took the money you gave me, and wrapped it up, and buried it in my yard. Here it is."

He thought his master would be pleased. But the man said, "You lazy, wicked servant! You know I like to get every cent I can out of anything I do. So you should have taken my money to the bank where it would have earned more money.

And with that, he took the one gold coin from the lazy servant and gave it to the one who had earned five. Then he threw the lazy one out of his house.

The Sheep and the Goats
Matthew 25:31—46

Jesus talked to his disciples while they sat together on the Mount of Olives, which is a hill above Jerusalem. He told them this story about himself.

When the king comes back, he will sit on his throne surrounded by angels. He will divide up the people, just the way a shepherd divides sheep from goats. The people he calls sheep will be on his right, and the people he calls goats will be on his left.

The king will turn to the people on his right, and say, "Come, you happy ones! You have pleased my Father. I was hungry, and you fed me. I was thirsty, and you gave me something to drink. I was a stranger, and you welcomed me. I had no clothes, and you gave me some. I was sick, and you visited me. I was in prison, and you came to see me."

The people will be very surprised. "When did we do all these things?" they will ask the king. "When did we see you hungry or thirsty? When did we help you?"

The king will say, "When you did it for even the most unimportant person, then you did it for me."

Then he will turn to the ones on his left hand. "But you!" he will say. "You saw me hungry and thirsty, poor and sick and in prison, and what did you do for me? Nothing!"

These people will cry, "But sir, when did we see you hungry or thirsty or needing clothes?"

"When you didn't do it for even the most unimportant person, then you did not do it for me."

A Woman Washes Jesus' Feet

Luke 7:36–50

One night Jesus went to dinner at the house of a Pharisee named Simon. When Jesus sat down, a woman came in and knelt by his feet. People knew that she was a sinner. She cried and washed his feet with her tears. Then she dried his feet with her long hair and rubbed them with perfumed oil.

Simon said to himself, "Doesn't Jesus know what sort of woman she is?"

Jesus knew what Simon was thinking. He said, "Simon, I want to tell you a story. Two men owed money to a man. One owed five hundred dollars. The other owed fifty dollars. When the man told them that they didn't have to pay the money back, which one was happier?"

"I guess the one who owed the most money," Simon answered.

"You're right," Jesus said.

Then he said, "Simon, when I came here, you didn't offer me water to wash. You did not give me a kiss or any oil for my head. But this woman washed my feet. She kissed them and rubbed perfumed oil on them. Her sins have been forgiven because she was so loving."

Jesus said to the woman, "Your sins are forgiven. You are saved by your faith. Go in peace."

Jesus Rides into Jerusalem
Mark 11:1–11

Jesus and his disciples were at the edge of the city of Jerusalem. They were going there for the Passover celebration. When they got to the Mount of Olives, Jesus told two of his disciples, "Go to that group of houses. You will find a colt tied up that nobody ever rode before. Tell the man who owns it that the Lord needs it. He will send it back right away."

So they went and found the colt and told the man what Jesus had said. They brought the colt to Jesus, and threw their capes over it for him to sit on. Then they started toward Jerusalem.

As they went, with the disciples walking and Jesus riding, people began to cry out, "Hosanna! Blessed is the one who comes in the name of the Lord! Hosanna in the highest!"

Others threw down green branches they had cut from the trees for Jesus and his followers to walk on. Some even threw down their coats and capes on the road in front of Jesus. There were crowds everywhere, full of joy because Jesus was there.

Jesus in the Temple
John 2:13–22

Jesus traveled in the temple in Jerusalem for the feast of Passover. Inside the temple, he found people selling sheep, cattle, and pigeons for sacrifices. He also saw moneychangers working.

He took some rope and knotted it to make a whip. Then he took it and drove all the moneychangers and sheep and cattle out. He turned over the moneychangers' tables and spilled coins everywhere. Jesus told the people who sold pigeons for sacrifice, "Take all these things out of here! You aren't going to make God's house a place for business!"

The people said, "Jesus, can you show us you have a right to do this?"

Jesus answered, "Tear this temple down, and I will build it up again in three days."

"What? It took forty-six years to build the temple. How could you build it in three days?"

Now when Jesus said "temple," he meant his own body. After he rose from the dead, his disciples remembered what he said.

The Last Supper
Matthew 26:17–20, 26–28; Luke 22:7–20

Jesus and his disciples went to Jerusalem for the feast of Passover. Jesus told Peter and John to go and get everything ready. They asked him, "Where do you want us to get it ready?"

"When you go into the city," said Jesus, "a man carrying a jar of water will meet you. Follow him into a house. Say to the owner that the Teacher asks where the room is where we are to eat our Passover supper. He will show you the room." They went as Jesus told them, and everything was just as he had said.

While they were sitting at the table that night, Jesus took some Passover bread. He thanked God for it. Then he broke the bread and said, "This is my body which is given for you. Do this in memory of me."

Jesus took the cup of wine. He passed it around and said, "Drink from this cup, all of you. This is my blood of the new covenant."

Jesus Washes His Disciples' Feet
John 13:1–17

When Jesus and his disciples came to the Passover supper, the devil was already in the heart of Judas Iscariot. Judas had decided to hand Jesus over to the temple police and the Roman soldiers. Jesus knew this. He also knew that soon he would return to God.

Jesus got up from the supper table and took off his outer robe. He tied a towel around his waist. He went around the table with a pan of water, washing his disciples' feet.

When he came to Peter, Peter jumped up and said, "No, Lord! I can't let you wash my feet!"

"If I don't, then you can't be part of me," said Jesus.

"Oh!" cried Peter. "Then wash my hands and my head too, so I can be part of you!"

"You don't need a bath," said Jesus. "All of you here are clean except one." He said this because he knew that Judas would betray him.

When Jesus finished, he put his robe back on and sat down. He said, "You call me Teacher and Lord, and that is good, because I am those things. Now if your Lord and Teacher washes your feet, you should do the same for each other. I have given you an example to copy. Treat each other the way I have treated you, and do for each other what I have done for you."

Jesus Goes to the Cross

Matthew 26:14–16, 33–75; 27:1–60; Mark 14:10–11, 26–72; 15; Luke 22:1–6, 33–71; 23:1–56

The chief priests and the temple lawyers were trying to find a way to arrest Jesus and kill him. One of the disciples, called Judas Iscariot, went secretly to the priests. Together they made a plan to capture Jesus.

After Jesus had eaten the Passover supper, he and his disciples sang a hymn. Then they walked to the Mount of Olives, a hill not far from Jerusalem. On the way Peter said, "Jesus, I will follow you everywhere. I would go to prison or die for you."

But Jesus told Peter, "Before the rooster crows in the morning, you will say three times that you do not know me."

When they got to the garden of Gethsemane, Jesus went a little way from them, and knelt under the trees. He prayed, "Father, if there is some way to change what is happening, change it! But what you want is what I will do."

Then an angel appeared to him and made him strong. He prayed harder and sweat fell from his forehead in great drops. Then he went back and found that his disciples were so tired that they had fallen into a deep sleep.

He was still calling them to wake up when Judas came. Judas was leading a crowd of people sent by the chief priests. Judas went up to Jesus and kissed him, so the men could know which one he was. Then the temple police grabbed Jesus and dragged him to the house of the high priest.

Peter followed them and waited outside near a fire in the courtyard. There was a servant girl there who said, "I think you are a friend of that Jesus."

"No," said Peter. "I don't know him."

Later a man said, "You are one of the disciples."

"You're wrong," said Peter. "I don't know him."

Finally a third person said, "I can tell you are from Galilee. You were with Jesus, weren't you?"

"I don't know what you're talking about!" shouted Peter. Just then a rooster crowed. Peter remembered Jesus' words to him, "You will say three times you do not know me."

Then Peter sat down and cried and cried.

Inside the high priest's house, the people who were holding Jesus hit him and made fun of him. They put a blindfold on him and called him names. They said, "If you're a prophet, tell us who hit you!"

Then the priests all came together and asked Jesus, "Are you the Christ, the Messiah? Tell us?"

"If I tell you, you won't believe me," said Jesus. "But from now on, the Son of man will sit at God's right hand."

"Are you God's son, then?" they asked.

"You said it yourselves," he answered.

"What more do we need?" they screamed. "We have heard it from his own mouth!"

Then they took him to Pontius Pilate, the Roman governor. After he talked to Jesus, Pilate told the priests, "I don't think that this man has committed a crime."

"He gets the people stirred up, everywhere he goes!" they said. "Even up in Galilee."

When Pilate found out that Jesus was from Galilee, he sent him to Herod, the ruler of Galilee. Herod was in Jerusalem for the Passover.

Herod asked Jesus many questions, but Jesus did not answer at all. Then Herod and his guards made fun of Jesus. They dressed Jesus up in a king's robe and sent him back to Pilate.

Pilate called the priests. "Jesus has not done anything to be killed for," he said. "I will have him whipped and then let him go."

"No!" they cried. "Crucify him!"

Pilate went and called to the crowd. "I always let one prisoner go during Passover. Shall I let Jesus go? Or the man named Barabbas, who is a murderer and who started a riot?"

"We want Barabbas!" they cried. "Crucify Jesus!"

So they led Jesus away to be crucified. On the way they found a man named

Simon, from the city of Cyrene, and made him help carry the heavy cross.

They came to a hill outside the city gates called Calvary or Golgotha, which means "the place of the skull." There the soldiers nailed Jesus to the cross.

Jesus prayed, "Father, forgive these men. They don't know what they are doing!"

They put a sign over Jesus' head that said, "This is the king of the Jews."

At about noon, the sky became dark and stayed dark until three o'clock in the afternoon. There was an earthquake, and the curtain in front of the holy place in the temple in Jerusalem tore in two.

Then Jesus cried in a loud voice, "Father, I give my spirit into your hands!" and he died.

The Roman captain who was there said, "He must have been the Son of God!"

A man from Arimathea named Joseph wrapped the body of Jesus in a clean sheet and took it to a new tomb in a garden.

The First Easter

John 20:1–18

Early on the sunday after Jesus was crucified, a woman named Mary of Magdala went to his tomb. She had followed Jesus and his disciples from Galilee.

When Mary got there it was still dark, but she could see that the stone was gone from the tomb! She ran to find Peter and John.

"They have taken Jesus away," she cried, "and we don't know where." The two men raced to the tomb. When they went inside, they saw the cloths that had wrapped Jesus, but that was all. They didn't understand that the Scriptures said that he must die and rise again.

Peter and John went back to their houses, but Mary stayed outside the tomb, crying. She stooped to look inside and saw two angels dressed in shining white.

"Why are you crying?" they asked.

"Because someone has taken Jesus away!" she sobbed.

Saying this, she turned around. Jesus was standing behind her, but she didn't recognize him.

"Woman, why are you crying?" asked Jesus. "Who are you looking for?"

She thought he was the gardener. "Sir," she said, "if you took Jesus away, tell me where he is."

Jesus said, "Mary."

She spun around and cried, "Teacher!"

"Don't hold on to me, Mary," he said. "I have not yet gone to my Father. Go tell my friends that I am returning to my Father and their Father, to my God and their God."

Then Mary went to the disciples and said, "I have seen the Lord!"

Thomas Sees the Risen Lord

John 20:19–29

On the Sunday after Jesus was crucified, the disciples were all together in a room with the doors locked. They were afraid of the temple police. Mary of Magdala had hurried back from the tomb to tell them that Jesus was alive again.

Suddenly Jesus himself was there. He stood in the room and said, "Peace be with you!"

He showed them the scars where he had been nailed to the cross. He showed them the place where a soldier's spear had cut his side. Then he said, "In the same way that my Father sent me, now I am sending you!" He breathed on them and said, "Let the Holy Spirit come into you. When you forgive people's sins, they are forgiven forever."

Thomas, one of the disciples, was not in the house when Jesus came. When the other disciples said, "We have seen the Lord," Thomas did not believe them.

"People can't rise from the dead," Thomas said. "I won't believe it until I see it for myself. I will have to see the scars and put my finger in the holes."

The next Sunday they were together again, and this time Thomas was with them. Jesus suddenly came into the room. He came even though the doors were shut.

"Peace be with you!" Jesus said. Turning to Thomas, he showed him his scars. He let Thomas touch the place where the nails had been. "Look, Thomas. Don't be faithless. Believe in me."

"My Lord and my God!" Thomas said to Jesus.

"You have seen me and believed, Thomas," said Jesus. "But happy are people who can believe without seeing."

The Road to Emmaus

Luke 24:13–35

On the day that Jesus rose from the dead, two of his friends walked to a small town called Emmaus. It was about seven miles from Jerusalem.

As they walked along, their faces gloomy, they talked about everything that had happened. Suddenly Jesus himself joined them, but they didn't recognize him. "What are you talking about?" Jesus asked.

One of them, named Cleopas, asked, "Are you the only person in the country who hasn't heard? Jesus, our teacher, was a great prophet. He did many miracles. We had hoped that he was the Messiah, the Christ, who would save Israel. But last Friday he was crucified. We were shocked when some of our women found his tomb empty. The women even said they had seen angels who told them that Jesus was alive. Some disciples went to his tomb and found it empty, too. Now we don't know what to think!"

"How foolish you are!" said Jesus. "Don't you know the prophets taught that these things would happen to the Christ, the Messiah?"

As they were walking, he talked about the law of Israel and the prophets, and what they said about him.

The two friends still did not know that this was Jesus. When they got to Emmaus, they begged him to eat with them. At the table he thanked God for the bread, broke it, and gave it to them. Suddenly they knew it was Jesus! But the next minute he disappeared.

Then they asked each other, "Wasn't it like a fire burning in us when he talked to us on the road?"

The two rushed back to Jerusalem. "We have seen the Lord!" they said.

Peter Goes Fishing

John 21:1–14

Jesus showed himself again to the disciples.

Peter, John, James, Thomas, Nathanael, and two other disciples went to Lake Tiberias. (This was another name for the Sea of Galilee.) Peter said, "I am going fishing."

"We'll go, too," said the others. They got in the boat and fished all night. But they didn't catch anything.

Just as the sun started to come up, they saw a man standing on the beach. They didn't know that it was Jesus.

"Did you catch anything?" he called.

"No," they answered.

"Put your net down on the right side of the boat," Jesus said. "You'll get something."

So they let their net down one more time. It was so full of fish that they could hardly haul it in.

One of the disciples said to Peter, "It's the Lord!"

When Peter heard who it was, he grabbed his robe, jumped into the water, and began wading ashore. The rest came in the boat, dragging the net full of fish.

When they got out on the beach, they saw a charcoal fire. Bread and fish were cooking on it.

"Bring some of those fish you caught," Jesus said. Peter dragged the net up on the beach. There were one hundred fifty-three large fish in the net. This was too many fish for the net, but it was still not torn.

Jesus said, "Now come and eat breakfast." He took the bread and the roasted fish and gave it to them. This was the third time that the disciples saw Jesus after he rose from the dead.

Jesus Goes to His Father

Acts 1:1–11

After Jesus rose from the dead, he came to be with his disciples many times.

Almost forty days after the first Easter, Jesus and his friends came together on the Mount of Olives, near Jerusalem. He talked to them about the kingdom of God.

"Do not leave Jerusalem after I am gone," he told the disciples. "Stay here until you receive the gift of the Holy Spirit. When John baptized you, it was with water. But before many days are past, you will be baptized again. You will be baptized with the Holy Spirit."

"Will that be the time when you bring back the kingdom of Israel?" they asked.

"Nobody except God knows this," he told them. "God decides when to do things. But I do know that the Holy Spirit will come to you soon. Then you will have power to tell the good news of my kingdom to all the countries of the world."

Jesus had stopped talking. But his friends were still looking at him. They watched as he was lifted up and disappeared in a cloud.

While they were still staring up at the sky, two men in shining white robes stood by them.

"You from Galilee," they said, "why are you staring up at the skies? This Jesus who was taken up into heaven will return in the same way that you saw him go!"

The Pentecost Story

Acts 1:4, 5, 13–14; 2:1–17, 22–47

It was Pentecost, a holiday in Israel. Pentecost came about fifty days after Jesus rose from the dead. Jesus' friends and disciples met together in a room in Jerusalem. Peter and James and John and the other disciples were there. So were Mary, Jesus' mother, and other men and women. Jesus had said that they should wait in Jerusalem for the baptism of the Holy Spirit.

Suddenly, as they sat together, they heard a sound like a great wind. It was rushing and roaring through the house, filling the room where they sat. Then small flames appeared like tongues of fire. These flames seemed to rest over each person there. They were all filled with the Holy Spirit. They began to talk in other languages that the Holy Spirit made them able to speak.

They ran into the streets, still speaking in these languages. Now there were many people from other countries who were in Jerusalem for the Pentecost holiday. They came from Iran and Iraq and Greece and Turkey and Egypt and Libya and Rome. But as the Christians spoke in the languages the Holy Spirit gave them, all the visitors heard the story of God in their own language!

The people asked each other, "What does this mean?"

Some of them said, "These people must be drunk to talk and act so strangely!"

But Peter spoke up. "We are not drunk at nine o'clock in the morning," he told them. " We are filled with God's Holy Spirit." Then he told them the story of Jesus Christ.

Three thousand of the people who listened were baptized that day. And they stayed faithful to what Jesus' disciples taught them. They went every day to visit the others, to pray, to hear the apostles teach, and to have Communion. And every day more and more people became Christians.

The Man at the Beautiful Gate

Acts 3:1–10

One afternoon at three o'clock Peter and John went to the temple to pray. As they were entering the temple, at the place called the Beautiful Gate, they saw a man who could not walk.

This man was born with crippled legs, so he could never learn to walk. He begged for money every day by the temple, because he could not work. When he saw Peter and John walking near him, he put out his hand and asked for money.

"Look at us!" said Peter. The man looked at them, expecting some money.

But Peter said, "I have no silver or gold to give you. But I have something else to give you." He took hold of the man's hand and said, "In the name of Jesus Christ of Nazareth, get up and walk!"

He pulled the lame man to his feet, and at once the man was healed. His legs and feet got strong. He walked. Then he leaped in the air. He went walking and leaping and praising God.

All the people saw the man, walking and jumping and full of joy. They knew he was the lame man by the gate. Then they were filled with wonder.

The Apostles in Jail

Acts 5:12–32

The disciples used to meet with the believers every day at Solomon's Portico, which was a sort of porch on the great temple.

People believed the disciples could heal the sick. They brought beds with sick people in them out to the road. Soon sick people were lying everywhere. They just hoped Peter's shadow would fall on them as he passed. And many were healed.

Then the high priest of the temple and his friends were jealous. They arrested the disciples and put them in jail.

But during the night an angel came and unlocked the doors. "Go to your regular place at the temple and tell people all about the new life Jesus has given you," said the angel. So the disciples did as they were told and went to the temple when the sun came up that morning.

The high priest and his friends called the Sanhedrin together. (The Sanhedrin was like a Congress for all of Israel.) They sent a messenger to the jail to fetch the prisoners.

When the messenger returned, he said, "The jail is locked tight. The guards are in their places. But the prisoners have disappeared!"

Then another man rushed in to say, "The men you're looking for are teaching at the temple!"

The temple officers went to get Peter and the others, but they were afraid to hurt them, because the people of the city would get very angry.

The high priest and the Sanhedrin said to the apostles, "We told you to stop teaching people about Jesus. Now look what you have done! People are blaming us for killing Jesus."

Peter and the apostles answered, "We must obey God, not just people. God raised Jesus from the dead after you crucified him. Now Jesus sits at God's right hand, to forgive sins. We know this to be true. So does the Holy Spirit, who comes from God to people who obey God."

Philip and the Man from Ethiopia
Acts 8:26–40

An angel came to Philip, one of the disciples. "Get up, Philip," said the angel. "Go down the desert road that leads from Jerusalem to Gaza."

Philip got up and began traveling. As he walked along, he saw a chariot. In it was a man from Ethiopia. He was the treasurer for the queen of Ethiopia.

"Go up to that man," the Holy Spirit told Philip. The disciple ran until he caught up with the chariot. He heard that the man was reading aloud the words of Isaiah, a prophet of Israel.

"Do you understand what you are reading?" asked Philip, walking beside the chariot.

"How can I understand it? I need a teacher," said the Ethiopian. He invited Philip to ride in the chariot. He hoped Philip could explain the prophet's words.

Now the part of the book of Isaiah that he was reading told about someone being killed like a sheep.

"Who is this person?" asked the man.

"That is the Christ, or Messiah," said Philip. "And he has already come!" Then Philip told him the good news of Jesus.

As the chariot rolled along, the Ethiopian saw a stream.

"Stop!" he said. "Here is water. Is there any reason why I can't be baptized right now?"

They got out of the chariot, and Philip baptized the man from Ethiopia in the name of Jesus.

The Road to Damascus

Acts 9:1–25

Saul was a Pharisee. He was very angry at all the people who believed in Jesus. He thought that Christians were disobeying God's law. He went around the country putting Christians in jail and trying to have them killed.

He got permission from the high priest to go to Damascus, a city in Syria. He planned to bring any Christians he found back to jail in Jerusalem.

While he was on the road to Damascus, he suddenly saw a bright light from heaven. It flashed around him, and he fell to the ground. Then he heard a voice saying, "Saul, Saul, why are you trying to hurt me?"

"Who are you, Lord?" asked Saul.

"I am Jesus. I am the one you are trying to hurt. Get up now and go into the city, and you will be told what to do."

The men who were traveling with Saul were too surprised to say a word. They heard the voice, but they did not see anyone.

When Saul got up, he opened his eyes but could not see anything! So the men with him had to lead him by the hand into Damascus. For three days he could not see or eat or drink anything.

Then the Lord sent a Christian named Ananias to Saul. Ananias touched Saul and said, "Brother Saul, you met Jesus on the road. Now he has sent me here so that you may see again and be filled with the Holy Spirit."

Suddenly Saul could see again! He was baptized right away. Then he ate something and soon felt stronger.

After that, Saul spent a few days with the disciples. He then went to the synagogues and preached, "Jesus is the Son of God!"

"Isn't this the man who hated the people who believed in Jesus?" people asked.

Saul upset many Jews in Damascus by persuading people that Jesus was the Messiah. But after many days some people wanted to shut Saul up by killing him. They watched the city gates day and night hoping to catch him. But Saul heard about the plan and escaped from Damascus in a basket tied to a rope. His new friends let it down over the city wall.

Saul was later called Paul. He became one of the greatest of the people who told the world about Jesus.

Peter Baptizes a Roman

Acts 10

Peter, the apostle of Jesus, went up onto the flat roof of the house at noon to say his prayers. Peter was hungry, but his dinner wasn't ready yet. While he was praying, he had a vision, a dream from God. He saw heaven open and something like a big sheet coming down. On the sheet were all kinds of animals, birds, snakes, and lizards. All of them were things that the law of Israel said people should not eat. They were called unclean.

"Get up and kill one of the animals and eat it," said a voice.

"Oh, no, Lord!" Peter answered. "These things are unclean. I have never eaten unclean things."

"You mustn't call something unclean when God has made it clean," said the voice.

Peter wondered what this vision meant.

Now there was a man named Cornelius. He was not a Jew. He was a Roman soldier who lived in Caesarea. He and his family were good people. They believed in God. One day, when Cornelius was praying, he saw an angel in a vision. Cornelius was frightened, but the angel said, "God has heard your prayers. God has accepted your gifts. Now send someone to Jaffa to bring back a man called Simon Peter." So Cornelius sent two slaves and a faithful soldier.

While Peter was still wondering about his vision, Cornelius' messengers arrived. Peter and some friends went with them to Caesarea. When they reached Cornelius' house, they found many people waiting.

Cornelius knelt in front of Peter, but Peter helped him up. "Stand up. I am only a man," Peter told him.

Peter saw how much Cornelius and his family believed in God. Then he knew what his vision about animals meant. God was not only for the Jews but for all people. So Peter told them all about Jesus Christ.

While he was talking, the Holy Spirit came to all who were listening. Then Cornelius and many others were baptized.

Peter Escapes from Jail

Acts 12:1–19

Herod was governor of Galilee. He hated the people who loved Jesus. He killed John's brother James. Then he had Peter arrested and put in jail.

Four squads of soldiers guarded Peter. While he was in the jail, all the Christians prayed hard for him.

After Passover, Herod decided to bring Peter out and put him on trial. The night before the trial Peter was asleep with two chains around him. A soldier stood on each side of him. Other soldiers watched the door to the jail.

Suddenly an angel came, and the jail was filled with light.

"Get up quickly!" the angel told Peter. The chains fell off, and Peter put on his belt and sandals and a warm cape and followed the angel. At first he thought he was dreaming. He passed by all the guards, and the big iron gate opened by itself. Peter found himself alone on the street.

"This is real!" Peter thought, "God has saved me!"

He went quickly to the house of Mary, John Mark's mother, and knocked on the door. A servant girl named Rhoda heard Peter calling through the door. She ran back to Mary. Mary and some other Christians were praying together.

"Peter is at the door!" she cried.

"You're crazy," everyone told her.

But Rhoda insisted. Finally they all went to the door. They saw that it really was Peter!

Paul and Barnabas Are Called Gods

Acts 14:8–17

Paul and Barnabas were apostles. They went from city to city, telling people the good news of Jesus Christ. In a city called Lystra they met a man who had never walked. His feet had been crippled since he was born.

Paul looked at the man and saw that he had faith to be made well. "Stand on your feet!" he said, and the man jumped up and walked.

The crowds of people who were around them said, "These men are really gods." They called Paul Hermes. They called Barnabas Zeus. (Hermes and Zeus were the names of Greek gods.) They brought oxen and flowers to the gates where Paul and Barnabas were.

"We will sacrifice the oxen to these gods!" they cried.

"Wait!" shouted Paul and Barnabas. "We are just men, like you. We came to bring you good news. You don't need to believe in these gods. Instead, there is the living God. God made heaven and earth and the oceans and everything in them!"

An Earthquake at the Jail

Acts 16:16–40

Paul and Silas were traveling around the country of Macedonia, telling people the good news of Jesus Christ. In the city of Philippi they saw a slave girl who had a wicked spirit inside her.

She used the spirit to tell fortunes. She followed Paul and Silas around yelling at them.

One day Paul stopped and turned around. He said to the wicked spirit, "In the name of Jesus, I command you to go away."

Her masters were angry. "We made much money from her fortunetelling!" they said. "Now she won't be able to tell fortunes."

These men dragged Peter and Silas to the rulers of the city. They said, "We heard Paul and Silas telling people to do things that were against the law."

Paul and Silas were beaten. Then they were locked in jail. The jailer was told to watch them carefully, so he chained their feet.

About midnight Paul and Silas were praying and singing hymns to God. Suddenly an earthquake rocked the jail. The doors and gates flew open. The chains fell off the prisoners.

The jailer woke up and saw the open doors. "The prisoners have escaped, and I will be punished for this!" he thought. He started to kill himself with his sword.

"Wait!" Paul shouted loudly. "Don't hurt yourself. We are all still here!"

The jailer was astonished. He called for lights and saw that Paul and Silas were still inside. Shaking with fear, he went in and knelt before them. "What must I do to be saved?" he asked them.

"Believe in the Lord Jesus. Then you and everyone in your house will be saved," they told the jailer. The jailer took them to his home. He washed their cuts. Then Paul and Silas told him and his servants and his family about Jesus. When they were finished, everyone in the house was baptized.

The next day the city rulers sent the police to the jailer. "Let these men go," they said.

"How can you treat us so badly?" asked Paul. "We are Roman citizens."

When the city rulers found this out, they were afraid. They came and apologized to them. Paul and Silas left the jail and visited some friends. Then they went to another city.

Paul in Athens

Acts 17:22–31

Paul was in Athens, a city in Greece. He preached the good news about Jesus Christ. He saw that the people there worshiped many gods. One day, he went to a large open square in the middle of the marketplace. This was called the Areopagus. All the people of Athens liked to come there to argue about ideas.

"People of Athens," Paul shouted, "I see that you have many gods and goddesses. And as I walked along today, I even saw an altar that said, 'To an unknown god.'

"This God does not have to be unknown any more! Our God made the earth and everything that is in it. Don't worship statues that are made from gold or silver. God is the one who gives us all life. God is not far from each one of us. Now God has given us new hope, by raising a man from the dead."

When some of the people heard about the resurrection, they made fun of Paul. But others said, "We want to know more about this." One of them was a woman named Damaris. Another was a man named Dionysius. With some others they became followers of Jesus.

The Holy City

Revelation 21

It was a number of years after Jesus ascended to heaven. A man named John lived on the island of Patmos.

One day John had a dream from God called a vision. He saw a new heaven and a new earth. The first heaven and earth were gone, and the ocean was gone, too. He saw a new city of Jerusalem, coming down from heaven, as beautiful as a bride on her wedding day.

A voice went out from God's throne that said, "Look! God and people live together now. God will be with the people. God will wipe away all the tears from their eyes. There will be no more sadness or pain in all the world."

And God said, "I make all things new."

The voice said to John in his vision, "Write all this down. I am Alpha and Omega, which is the beginning and the end. I will give the water of life to those who are thirsty. I will be their God, and they will be my children."

Lectionary Tables

The following tables relate the stories in this book to the readings in four lectionaries: the Episcopal lectionary in the Book of Common Prayer, the Roman Catholic lectionary, the Methodist lectionary, and the Common Lectionary. If one of the readings for a given Sunday is included among the stories of this book, the title of the story is listed with that Sunday. If none of the readings is included among the stories of this book, another story, which illustrates concepts of the lectionary readings or is clearly related to the lectionary readings, is listed with the title of the story in parentheses.

Episcopal

	Year A	Year B	Year C
First Sunday of Advent	(The Sheep and the Goats 149) (Being Ready for God 145)	Being Ready for God 145	(Ten Women with Their Lamps 146)
Second Sunday of Advent	John the Baptist Preaches 92	John the Baptist Preaches 92	(The Birth of John the Baptist 83)
Third Sunday of Advent	The Desert Shall Bloom 70	The Lion and the Lamb 72	John the Baptist Preaches 92
Fourth Sunday of Advent	(The Annunciation to Mary 84)	The Annunciation to Mary 84	The Annunciation to Mary 84
Christmas through the Feast of the Epiphany	The Birth of Jesus 86 The Coming of the Wise Men 88 (The Presentation of the Baby Jesus in the Temple 89) The Escape to Egypt 90 The Boy Jesus in the Temple 91	The Birth of Jesus 86 The Coming of the Wise Men 88 (The Presentation of the Baby Jesus in the Temple 89) The Escape to Egypt 90 The Boy Jesus in the Temple 91	The Birth of Jesus 86 The Coming of the Wise Men 88 (The Presentation of the Baby Jesus in the Temple 89) The Escape to Egypt 90 The Boy Jesus in the Temple 91
First Sunday after Epiphany	Jesus Is Baptized 94	Jesus Is Baptized 94	Jesus Is Baptized 94
Second Sunday after Epiphany	(A Wedding at Cana 99)	God Calls Samuel 51	A Wedding at Cana 99
Third Sunday after Epiphany	Fishing for People 97	(The Story of Jonah 78) Fishing for People 97	Jesus Teaches in the Synagogue 96
Fourth Sunday after Epiphany	The Beatitudes: Jesus Talks about Blessings 98	(Elijah and the Prophets of Baal 61)	(Naaman the Leper 68)
Presentation of Our Lord	The Presentation of the Baby Jesus in the Temple 89	The Presentation of the Baby Jesus in the Temple 89	The Presentation of the Baby Jesus in the Temple 89
Fifth Sunday after Epiphany	(The Sower 116) (The Lord's Prayer 122)	Elisha Visits a Family 66	(The Call of Isaiah 69) Fishing for People 97
Sixth Sunday after Epiphany	(The Ten Commandments 32)	Naaman the Leper 68	The Beatitudes: Jesus Talks about Blessings 98
Seventh Sunday after Epiphany	(Jesus Talks about the Law of Israel 137) (The Good Samaritan 119)	A Man Who Could Not Walk 104	(Joseph Forgives His Brothers 18)

Episcopal continued

	Year A	Year B	Year C
Eighth Sunday after Epiphany	Lilies of the Field 100	(A Wedding at Cana 99)	Can the Blind Lead the Blind? 110
Last Sunday after Epiphany	The Transfiguration of Jesus 140	Elijah at the Mountain of God 63 (Chariots of Fire 65) The Transfiguration of Jesus 140	The Face of Moses Shines 36 The Transfiguration of Jesus 140
First Sunday in Lent	The Garden of Eden 4 God Makes the First Man and Woman 3 The Temptation of Jesus 95	Noah and the Rainbow Covenant 5 The Temptation of Jesus 95	The Temptation of Jesus 95
Second Sunday in Lent	God Calls Abram 8	(Sarah and Abraham 10)	God's Covenant with Abram 9
Third Sunday in Lent	Water from the Rock 31	The Ten Commandments 32 Jesus in the Temple 152	Moses and the Burning Bush 23
Fourth Sunday in Lent	The Anointing of David 52 The Man Who Was Born Blind 114	(The Plagues and Passover 25) The Babylonian Exile and Return 74 Feeding Five Thousand People 112	Joshua Crosses the Jordan 43 The Prodigal Son 126
Fifth Sunday in Lent	The Valley of Dry Bones 75 Jesus and His Friend Lazarus 141	(Crossing the Red Sea 27)	(The Plagues and Passover 25) (Crossing the Red Sea 27)
Palm Sunday *Maundy Thursday* *Good Friday*	Jesus Rides into Jerusalem 151 Jesus in the Temple 152 The Last Supper 153 Jesus Washes His Disciples' Feet 154 Jesus Goes to the Cross 155	Jesus Rides into Jerusalem 151 Jesus in the Temple 152 The Last Supper 153 Jesus Washes His Disciples' Feet 154 Jesus Goes to the Cross 155	Jesus Rides into Jerusalem 151 Jesus in the Temple 152 The Last Supper 153 Jesus Washes His Disciples' Feet 154 Jesus Goes to the Cross 155

Episcopal continued

	Year A	Year B	Year C
Proper 5 *June 5–11*	Jesus Asks Matthew to Follow Him 102	The Garden of Eden 4	(Elijah and the Widow's Bread 59)
Proper 6 *June 12–18*	The Twelve Disciples 103	(Daniel in the Lions' Den 76) The Mustard Seed 106	A Woman Washes Jesus' Feet 150
Proper 7 *June 19–25*	(The Garden of Eden 4)	Jesus Calms the Storm 107	(David Brings the Ark to Jerusalem 156)
Proper 8 *June 26–July 2*	(David and Goliath 54) (Elisha Visits a Family 66)	Jesus and the Little Girl 113	Elijah at the Mountain of God 63
Proper 9 *July 3–9*	(Jesus Rides into Jerusalem 151)	Jesus Teaches in the Synagogue 96	Jesus Sends Seventy-Two People to Teach 118
Proper 10 *July 10–16*	The Sower 116	The Twelve Disciples 103	The Good Samaritan 119
Proper 11	The Wheat and the Weeds 117	Feeding Five Thousand People 112	Sarah and Abraham 10
July 17–23			Mary and Martha 120
Proper 12 *July 24–30*	The Mustard Seed 106 (Daniel in the Lions' Den 76)	Chariots of Fire 65 Jesus Walks on Water 123	The Lord's Prayer 122
Proper 13	Feeding Five Thousand People 112	Manna and Quails 29	(Lilies of the Field 100)
July 31–August 6			
Transfiguration of Our Lord *August 6*	The Transfiguration of Jesus 140	The Transfiguration of Jesus 140	The Transfiguration of Jesus 140
Proper 14 *August 7–13*	(Elijah at the Mountain of God 63) Jesus Walks on Water 123	(Spies in the Promised Land 41) (Elijah at the Mountain of God 63) (Lilies of the Field 100)	God's Covenant with Abram 9

Episcopal continued

	Year A	Year B	Year C
Proper 15 August 14–20	(The Story of Ruth 48)	(The Last Supper 153)	Jeremiah in the Well 73
Proper 16 August 21–27	Peter Is Given His Name 129 (Jesus Goes to the Cross 155)	Joshua Writes the Covenant 47	(The Sheep and the Goats 149)
Proper 17 August 28–September 3	(Elijah and the Widow's Bread 59) (The Widow's Penny 144)	(God's Law for Israel 37) (The Battle of Jericho 45)	Invited to a Feast 124
Proper 18 September 4–10	(The Valley of Dry Bones 75)	(The Lame Man at the Pool 108) Jesus Heals a Deaf Man 128	(Hannah and Samuel 49)
Proper 19 September 11–17	The Wicked Servant 130	(The Good Samaritan 119)	The Golden Calf 34 The Lost Sheep 125
Proper 20 September 18–24	The Story of Jonah 79 The Workers in the Vineyard 131	(The Pharisee and the Tax Collector 138)	(Joseph Becomes a Slave 14)
Proper 21 September 25–October 1	Two Sons 134	The People Complain to Moses 38 (The Man Who Was Born Blind 114)	(Joseph Forgives His Brothers 18)
Proper 22 October 2–8	(Joseph Becomes a Slave 14)	God Makes the First Man and Woman 3	(Daniel in the Lions' Den 76)
Proper 23 October 9–15	(Joseph and the Meaning of Dreams 16) Invitations to a Wedding 135	(The Birth of Moses 21)	The Story of Ruth 48 Jesus Heals Ten Men 133
Proper 24 October 16–22	(Joseph Forgives His Brothers 18) (The Babylonian Exile and Return 74)	(The Last Supper 153) (Jesus Washes His Disciples' Feet 154)	Jacob Becomes Israel 12 The Poor Woman and the Judge 136
Proper 25 October 23–29	(The Good Samaritan 119) Jesus Talks about the Law of Israel 137	The Blind Beggar 143	The Pharisee and the Tax Collector 138

Roman Catholic

	Year A	Year B	Year C
First Sunday of Advent	(The Sheep and the Goats 149) Being Ready for God 145	Being Ready for God 145	(Ten Women with Their Lamps 146)
Second Sunday of Advent	John the Baptist Preaches 92 (The Lion and the Lamb 72)	John the Baptist Preaches 92	(The Birth of John the Baptist 83)
Third Sunday of Advent	The Desert Shall Bloom 70	(The Lion and the Lamb 72)	John the Baptist Preaches 92
Fourth Sunday of Advent	(The Annunciation to Mary 84)	The Annunciation to Mary 84	(The Annunciation to Mary 84)
Christmas through the Feast of the Epiphany	The Birth of Jesus 86 The Coming of the Wise Men 88 (The Presentation of the Baby Jesus in the Temple 89) The Escape to Egypt 90 (The Boy Jesus in the Temple 91)	The Birth of Jesus 86 The Coming of the Wise Men 88 The Presentation of the Baby Jesus in the Temple 89 The Escape to Egypt 90 (The Boy Jesus in the Temple 91)	The Birth of Jesus 86 The Coming of the Wise Men 88 (The Presentation of the Baby Jesus in the Temple 89) The Escape to Egypt 90 The Boy Jesus in the Temple 91
Baptism of the Lord	Jesus Is Baptized 94 Peter Baptizes a Roman 169	Jesus Is Baptized 94 Peter Baptizes a Roman 169	Jesus Is Baptized 94 Peter Baptizes a Roman 169
Second Sunday of the Year	(A Wedding at Cana 99)	God Calls Samuel 51	A Wedding at Cana 99
Third Sunday of the Year	Fishing for People 97	The Story of Jonah 78 Fishing for People 97	Jesus Teaches in the Synagogue 96
Fourth Sunday of the Year	The Beatitudes: Jesus Talks about Blessings 98	(Elijah and the Prophets of Baal 61)	(Naaman the Leper 68)
Fifth Sunday of the Year	(The Sower 116) (The Lord's Prayer 122)	(Elisha Visits a Family 66)	The Call of Isaiah 69 Fishing for People 97
Sixth Sunday of the Year	(The Ten Commandments 32)	(Naaman the Leper 68)	The Beatitudes: Jesus Talks about Blessings 98
Seventh Sunday of the Year	Jesus Talks about the Law of Israel 137 (The Good Samaritan 119)	A Man Who Could Not Walk 104	(Joseph Forgives His Brothers 18)

Roman Catholic continued

	Year A	Year B	Year C
Eighth Sunday of the Year	Lilies of the Field 100	(A Wedding at Cana 99)	Can the Blind Lead the Blind? 110
First Sunday of Lent	The Garden of Eden 4 God Makes the First Man and Woman 3 The Temptation of Jesus 95	Noah and the Rainbow Covenant 5 The Temptation of Jesus 95	The Temptation of Jesus 95
Second Sunday of Lent	God Calls Abram 8 The Transfiguration of Jesus 140	(Sarah and Abraham 10) The Transfiguration of Jesus 140	God's Covenant with Abram 9 The Transfiguration of Jesus 140
Third Sunday of Lent	Water from the Rock 31	The Ten Commandments 32 Jesus in the Temple 152	Moses and the Burning Bush 23
Fourth Sunday of Lent	The Anointing of David 52 The Man Who was Born Blind 114	(The Plagues and Passover 25) The Babylonian Exile and Return 74 (Feeding 5000 People 112)	(Joshua Crosses the Jordan 43) The Prodigal Son 126
Fifth Sunday of Lent	The Valley of Dry Bones 75 Jesus and His Friend Lazarus 141	(Crossing the Red Sea 27)	(The Plagues and Passover 25) (Crossing the Red Sea 27)
Palm Sunday *Holy Thursday* *Good Friday*	Jesus Rides into Jerusalem 151 Jesus in the Temple 152 The Last Supper 153 Jesus Washes His Disciples' Feet 154 Jesus Goes to the Cross 155	Jesus Rides into Jerusalem 151 Jesus in the Temple 152 The Last Supper 153 Jesus Washes His Disciples' Feet 154 Jesus Goes to the Cross 155	Jesus Rides into Jerusalem 151 Jesus in the Temple 152 The Last Supper 153 Jesus Washes His Disciples' Feet 154 Jesus Goes to the Cross 155

Roman Catholic continued

	Year A	Year B	Year C
Easter Vigil and Easter Day	God Makes the Universe 1 Crossing the Red Sea 27 (The Babylonian Exile and Return 74) (The Valley of Dry Bones 75) The First Easter 158	God Makes the Universe 1 Crossing the Red Sea 27 (The Babylonian Exile and Return 74) (The Valley of Dry Bones 75) The First Easter 158	God Makes the Universe 1 Crossing the Red Sea 27 (The Babylonian Exile and Return 74) (The Valley of Dry Bones 75) The First Easter 158
Second Sunday of Easter	Thomas Sees the Risen Lord 161	Thomas Sees the Risen Lord 161	(The Apostles in Jail 166) Thomas Sees the Risen Lord 161
Third Sunday of Easter	The Road to Emmaus 161	(The Man at the Beautiful Gate 165)	Peter Goes Fishing 162 (The Road to Damascus 168) The Apostles in Jail 166
Fourth Sunday of Easter	The Good Shepherd 121	The Good Shepherd 121	(The Good Shepherd 121) (Philip and the Man from Ethiopia 167)
Fifth Sunday of Easter	(The Road to Damascus 168)	(Philip and the Man from Ethiopia 167)	(Peter Escapes from Jail 170) The Holy City 174
Sixth Sunday of Easter	(Paul Preaches in Athens 173) (Peter Escapes from Jail 170)	Peter Baptizes a Roman 169	Paul and Barnabas Are Called Gods 171
Ascension Day	Jesus Goes to His Father 163	Jesus Goes to His Father 163	Jesus Goes to His Father 163
Seventh Sunday of Easter	(Jesus Goes to His Father 163)	(Jesus Goes to His Father 163)	(Jesus Goes to His Father 163) (An Earthquake at the Jail 172)
Pentecost	The Pentecost Story 164	The Pentecost Story 164	(The Tower of Babel 7) The Pentecost Story 164
Trinity Sunday	(God Makes the Universe 1)	(Moses and the Burning Bush 23)	(The Call of Isaiah 69)
Ninth Sunday of the Year	A House Built on Rock 101	Picking Grain on the Sabbath 105	The Centurion's Servant 111

Roman Catholic   continued

	Year A	Year B	Year C
Tenth Sunday of the Year	Jesus Asks Matthew to Follow Him 102	The Garden of Eden 4	(Elijah and the Widow's Bread 59)
Eleventh Sunday of the Year	The Twelve Disciples 103	(Daniel in the Lions' Den 76) The Mustard Seed 106	A Woman Washes Jesus' Feet 150
Twelfth Sunday of the Year	(The Garden of Eden 4)	Jesus Calms the Storm 107	(David Brings the Ark to Jerusalem 156) Peter Is Given His Name 129
Thirteenth Sunday of the Year	(David and Goliath 54) Elisha Visits a Family 66	Jesus and the Little Girl 113	Elijah at the Mountain of God 63
Fourteenth Sunday of the Year	(Jesus Rides into Jerusalem 151)	Jesus Teaches in the Synagogue 96	Jesus Sends Seventy-Two People to Teach 118
Fifteenth Sunday of the Year	The Sower 116	The Twelve Disciples 103	The Good Samaritan 119
Sixteenth Sunday of the Year	The Wheat and the Weeds 117	Feeding Five Thousand People 112	Sarah and Abraham 10 Mary and Martha 120
Seventeenth Sunday of the Year	(The Mustard Seed 106) (Daniel in the Lions' Den 76)	Feeding Five Thousand People 112 (Chariots of Fire 65)	The Lord's Prayer 122
Eighteenth Sunday of the Year	Feeding Five Thousand People 112	Manna and Quails 29	(Lilies of the Field 100)
Nineteenth Sunday of the Year	Elijah at the Mountain of God 63 Jesus Walks on Water 123	(Spies in the Promised Land 41) Elijah at the Mountain of God 63 (Lilies of the Field 100)	(God's Covenant with Abram 9)
Twentieth Sunday of the Year	(The Story of Ruth 48)	(The Last Supper 153)	Jeremiah in the Well 73

Roman Catholic continued

	Year A	Year B	Year C
Twenty-first Sunday of the Year	Peter Is Given His Name 129 (Jesus Goes to the Cross 155)	Joshua Writes the Covenant 47	(The Sheep and the Goats 149)
Twenty-second Sunday of the Year	(Elijah and the Widow's Bread 59) (The Widow's Penny 144)	(God's Law for Israel 37) (The Battle of Jericho 45)	Invited to a Feast 124
Twenty-third Sunday of the Year	(The Valley of Dry Bones 75)	The Desert Shall Bloom 71 (The Lame Man at the Pool 108) Jesus Heals a Deaf Man 128	(Hannah and Samuel 49)
Twenty-fourth Sunday of the Year	The Wicked Servant 130	Peter Is Given His Name 129 (The Good Samaritan 119)	The Golden Calf 34 The Lost Sheep 125 The Prodigal Son 126
Twenty-fifth Sunday of the Year	(The Story of Jonah 79) The Workers in the Vineyard 131	(The Pharisee and the Tax Collector 138	(Joseph Becomes a Slave 14)
Twenty-sixth Sunday of the Year	Two Sons 134	The People Complain to Moses 38 (The Man Who Was Born Blind 114)	(Joseph Forgives His Brothers 18)
Twenty-seventh Sunday of the Year	(Joseph Becomes a Slave 14)	God Makes the First Man and Woman 3	(Daniel in the Lion's Den 76)
Twenty-eighth Sunday of the Year	(Joseph and the Meaning of Dreams 16) Invitations to a Wedding 135	(The Birth of Moses 21)	Jesus Heals Ten Men 133
Twenty-ninth Sunday of the Year	(Joseph Forgives His Brothers 18) (The Babylonian Exile and Return 74)	(The Last Supper 153) Jesus Washes His Disciples' Feet 154)	The Poor Woman and the Judge 136
Thirtieth Sunday of the Year	(The Good Samaritan 119) Jesus Talks about the Law of Israel 137	The Blind Beggar 143	The Pharisee and the Tax Collector 138

Roman Catholic continued

	Year A	Year B	Year C
Thirty-first Sunday of the Year	(Jesus Washes His Disciples' Feet *154*)	(The Good Samaritan *119*) Jesus Talks about the Law of Israel *137*	Zacchaeus in the Sycamore Tree *139*
All Saints' Day	The Beatitudes: Jesus Talks about Blessings *98*	The Beatitudes: Jesus Talks about Blessings *98*	The Beatitudes: Jesus Talks about Blessings *98*
Thirty-second Sunday of the Year	Ten Women with Their Lamps *146*	Elijah and the Widow's Bread *59* The Widow's Penny *144*	(Moses and the Burning Bush *23*)
Thirty-third Sunday of the Year	A Story about Money *148*	(A Story about Money *148*)	(The Tabernacle *39*) (Solomon Builds God's Temple *57*)
Last Sunday of the Year; Feast of Christ the King	The Sheep and the Goats *149*	(The Sheep and the Goats *149*)	(Jesus Rides into Jerusalem *151*)

Methodist

	Year A	Year B	Year C
First Sunday in Advent	(The Sheep and the Goats 149)	Being Ready for God 145	(Ten Women with Their Lamps 146)
Second Sunday in Advent	John the Baptist Preaches 92	John the Baptist Preaches 92	(The Birth of John the Baptist 83)
Third Sunday in Advent	The Desert Shall Bloom 70	(The Lion and the Lamb 72)	John the Baptist Preaches 92
Fourth Sunday in Advent	(The Annunciation to Mary 84)	The Annunciation to Mary 84	The Annunciation to Mary 84
Christmas through the Epiphany	The Birth of Jesus 86 The Coming of the Wise Men 88 (The Presentation of the Baby Jesus in the Temple 89) The Escape to Egypt 90 (The Boy Jesus in the Temple 91)	The Birth of Jesus 86 The Coming of the Wise Men 88 The Presentation of the Baby Jesus in the Temple 89 (The Escape to Egypt 90) (The Boy Jesus in the Temple 91)	The Birth of Jesus 86 The Coming of the Wise Men 88 (The Presentation of the Baby Jesus in the Temple 89) The Escape to Egypt 90 The Boy Jesus in the Temple 91
First Sunday after Epiphany	Jesus Is Baptized 94	Jesus Is Baptized 94	Jesus Is Baptized 94
Second Sunday after Epiphany	(A Wedding at Cana 99)	God Calls Samuel 51	A Wedding at Cana 99
Third Sunday after Epiphany	Fishing for People 97	The Story of Jonah 78 Fishing for People 97	Jesus Teaches in the Synagogue 96
Fourth Sunday after Epiphany	The Beatitudes: Jesus Talks about Blessings 98	(Elijah and the Prophets of Baal 61)	(Naaman the Leper 68)
Fifth Sunday after Epiphany	(The Sower 116) (The Lord's Prayer 122)	(Elisha Visits a Family 66)	The Call of Isaiah 69 Fishing for People 97
Sixth Sunday after Epiphany	(The Ten Commandments 32)	Naaman the Leper 68	The Beatitudes: Jesus Talks about Blessings 98
Seventh Sunday after Epiphany	(Jesus Talks about the Law of Israel 137) (The Good Samaritan 119)	A Man Who Could Not Walk 104	(Joseph Forgives His Brothers 18)
Eighth Sunday after Epiphany	Lilies of the Field 100	(A Wedding at Cana 99)	Can the Blind Lead the Blind? 110

Methodist continued

	Year A	Year B	Year C
Last Sunday after Epiphany	The Transfiguration of Jesus *140*	Chariots of Fire *65* The Transfiguration of Jesus *140*	(The Face of Moses Shines *36*) The Transfiguration of Jesus *140*
First Sunday in Lent	The Garden of Eden *4* The Temptation of Jesus *95*	Noah and the Rainbow Covenant *5* The Temptation of Jesus *95*	The Temptation of Jesus *95*
Second Sunday in Lent	God Calls Abram *8*	(Sarah and Abraham *10*)	God's Covenant with Abram *9*
Third Sunday in Lent	Water from the Rock *31*	The Ten Commandments *32* Jesus in the Temple *152*	Moses and the Burning Bush *23*
Fourth Sunday in Lent	The Anointing of David *52* The Man Who Was Born Blind *114*	(The Plagues and Passover *25*) The Babylonian Exile and Return *74*	Joshua Crosses the Jordan *43* The Prodigal Son *126*
Fifth Sunday in Lent	The Valley of Dry Bones *75* Jesus and His Friend Lazarus *141*	(Crossing the Red Sea *27*)	(The Plagues and Passover *25*) (Crossing the Red Sea *27*)
Passion/Palm Sunday *Maundy Thursday* *Good Friday*	Jesus Rides into Jerusalem *151* Jesus in the Temple *152* The Last Supper *153* Jesus Washes His Disciples' Feet *154* Jesus Goes to the Cross *155*	Jesus Rides into Jerusalem *151* Jesus in the Temple *152* The Last Supper *153* Jesus Washes His Disciples' Feet *154* Jesus Goes to the Cross *155*	Jesus Rides into Jerusalem *151* Jesus in the Temple *152* The Last Supper *153* Jesus Washes His Disciples' Feet *154* Jesus Goes to the Cross *155*
Easter Vigil and Easter Day	God Makes the Universe *1* Crossing the Red Sea *27* (The Babylonian Exile and Return *74*) (The Valley of Dry Bones *75*) The First Easter *158*	God Makes the Universe *1* Crossing the Red Sea *27* (The Babylonian Exile and Return *74*) (The Valley of Dry Bones *75*) The First Easter *158*	God Makes the Universe *1* Crossing the Red Sea *27* (The Babylonian Exile and Return *74*) (The Valley of Dry Bones *75*) The First Easter *158*
Second Sunday of Easter	Thomas Sees the Risen Lord *159*	Thomas Sees the Risen Lord *159*	The Apostles in Jail *166* Thomas Sees the Risen Lord *159*

Methodist continued

	Year A	Year B	Year C
Third Sunday of Easter	The Road to Emmaus 161	(The Man at the Beautiful Gate 165)	Peter Goes Fishing 162 The Road to Damascus 168
Fourth Sunday of Easter	The Good Shepherd 121	The Good Shepherd 121	(The Good Shepherd 121) (Philip and the Man from Ethiopia 167)
Fifth Sunday of Easter	(The Road to Damascus 168)	Philip and the Man from Ethiopia 167	(Peter Escapes from Jail 170) The Holy City 174
Sixth Sunday of Easter	Paul Preaches in Athens 173 (Peter Escapes from Jail 170)	(Peter Baptizes a Roman 169)	Paul and Barnabas Are Called Gods 174
Seventh Sunday of Easter	Jesus Goes to His Father 163	Jesus Goes to His Father 163	Jesus Goes to His Father 163 An Earthquake at the Jail 172
Pentecost	The Pentecost Story 164	The Pentecost Story 164	The Tower of Babel 7 The Pentecost Story 164
Trinity Sunday	God Makes the Universe 1	(Moses and the Burning Bush 23)	(The Call of Isaiah 69)
May 22–28	Lilies of the Field 100	(A Wedding at Cana 99)	Can the Blind Lead the Blind? 110
May 29–June 4	A House Built on Rock 101	The Ten Commandments 32 Picking Grain on the Sabbath 105	The Centurion's Servant 111
June 5–11	Jesus Asks Matthew to Follow Him 102	The Garden of Eden 4	(Elijah and the Widow's Bread 59)
June 12–18	The Twelve Disciples 103	(Daniel in the Lions' Den 76) The Mustard Seed 106	A Woman Washes Jesus' Feet 150
June 19–25	(The Garden of Eden 4)	Jesus Calms the Storm 107	(David Brings the Ark to Jerusalem 156)
June 26–July 2	(David and Goliath 54) Elisha Visits a Family 66	Jesus and the Little Girl 107	Elijah at the Mountain of God 63

Methodist

continued

	Year A	Year B	Year C
July 3–9	(Jesus Rides into Jerusalem *151*)	Jesus Teaches in the Synagogue *96*	Jesus Sends Seventy-Two People to Teach *118*
July 10–16	The Sower *116*	The Twelve Disciples *103*	The Good Samaritan *119*
July 17–23	The Wheat and the Weeds *117*	Feeding Five Thousand People *112*	Sarah and Abraham *10* Mary and Martha *120*
July 24–30	The Mustard Seed *106* (Daniel in the Lions' Den *76*)	(Chariots of Fire *65*) (Jesus Walks on Water *123*)	The Lord's Prayer *122*
July 31–August 6	Feeding Five Thousand People *112*	Manna and Quails *29*	(Lilies of the Field *100*)
August 7–13	Elijah at the Mountain of God *63* Jesus Walks on Water *123*	Elijah at the Mountain of God *63* (Lilies of the Field *100*)	God's Covenant with Abram *9*
August 14–20	(The Story of Ruth *48*)	(The Last Supper *153*)	Jeremiah in the Well *73*
August 21–27	Peter Is Given His Name *129* (Jesus Goes to the Cross *155*)	Joshua Writes the Covenant *47*	(The Sheep and the Goats *149*)
August 28–September 3	(Elijah and the Widow's Bread *59*) (The Widow's Penny *144*)	(God's Law for Israel *37*) (The Battle of Jericho *45*)	Invited to a Feast *124*
September 4–10	(The Valley of Dry Bones *75*)	(The Lame Man at the Pool *108*) Jesus Heals a Deaf Man *128*	(Hannah and Samuel *49*)
September 11–17	The Wicked Servant *130*	(The Good Samaritan *119*)	The Golden Calf *34* The Lost Sheep *125*
September 18–24	The Workers in the Vineyard *131*	(The Pharisee and the Tax Collector *138*)	(Joseph Becomes a Slave *14*)
September 25–October 1	Two Sons *134*	The People Complain to Moses *38* (The Man Who Was Born Blind *114*)	(Joseph Forgives His Brothers *18*)

Methodist continued

	Year A	Year B	Year C
October 2–8	(Joseph Becomes a Slave 14)	God Makes the First Man and Woman 3	(Daniel in the Lions' Den 76)
October 9–15	(Joseph and the Meaning of Dreams 16) Invitations to a Wedding 135	(The Birth of Moses 21)	The Story of Ruth 48 Jesus Heals Ten Men 133
October 16–22	(Joseph Forgives His Brothers 18) (The Babylonian Exile and Return 74)	(The Last Supper 153) (Jesus Washes His Disciples' Feet 154)	Jacob Becomes Israel 12 The Poor Woman and the Judge 136
October 23–29	(The Good Samaritan 119) Jesus Talks about the Law of Israel 137	The Blind Beggar 143	The Pharisee and the Tax Collector 138
October 30–November 5	(Jesus Washes His Disciples' Feet 154)	(The Good Samaritan 119) Jesus Talks about the Law of Israel 137	Zacchaeus in the Sycamore Tree 139
All Saints' Day	The Beatitudes: Jesus Talks About Blessings 98	The Beatitudes: Jesus Talks About Blessings 98	The Beatitudes: Jesus Talks About Blessings 98
November 6–12	Ten Women with Their Lamps 146	Elijah and the Widow's Bread 59 The Widow's Penny 144	(Moses and the Burning Bush 23)
November 13–19	A Story about Money 148	(A Story about Money 148)	(The Tabernacle 39) (Solomon Builds God's Temple 57)
November 20–26; Feast of Christ the King	The Sheep and the Goats 149	(The Sheep and the Goats 149)	(Jesus Rides into Jerusalem 151)

The Common Lectionary

	Year A	Year B	Year C
First Sunday of Advent	(The Sheep and the Goats 149) Being Ready for God 145	Being Ready for God 145	(Ten Women with Their Lamps 146) (Being Ready for God 145)
Second Sunday of Advent	John the Baptist Preaches 92 (The Lion and the Lamb 72)	John the Baptist Preaches 92	(The Birth of John the Baptist 83)
Third Sunday of Advent	The Desert Shall Bloom 70	(The Lion and the Lamb 72)	John the Baptist Preaches 92
Fourth Sunday of Advent	(The Annunciation to Mary 84)	The Annunciation to Mary 84	The Annunciation to Mary 84
Christmas through the Feast of Epiphany	The Birth of Jesus 86 The Coming of the Wise Men 88 (The Presentation of the Baby Jesus in the Temple 89) The Escape to Egypt 90 (The Boy Jesus in the Temple 91)	The Birth of Jesus 86 The Coming of the Wise Men 88 The Presentation of the Baby Jesus in the Temple 89 The Escape to Egypt 90 (The Boy Jesus in the Temple 91)	The Birth of Jesus 86 The Coming of the Wise Men 88 (The Presentation of the Baby Jesus in the Temple 89) The Escape to Egypt 90 The Boy Jesus in the Temple 91
Baptism of the Lord / First Sunday after Epiphany	Jesus Is Baptized 94 Peter Baptizes a Roman 169	God Makes the Universe 1 Jesus Is Baptized 94	Jesus Is Baptized 94
Second Sunday after Epiphany	(A Wedding at Cana 99)	God Calls Samuel 51	A Wedding at Cana 99
Third Sunday after Epiphany	Fishing for People 97	The Story of Jonah 78 Fishing for People 97	Jesus Teaches in the Synagogue 96
Fourth Sunday after Epiphany	The Beatitudes: Jesus Talks about Blessings 98	(Elijah and the Prophets of Baal 61)	Jesus Teaches in the Synagogue 96 (Naaman the Leper 68)
Fifth Sunday after Epiphany	(The Sower 116) (The Lord's Prayer 122)	(Elisha Visits a Family 66)	The Call of Isaiah 69 Fishing for People 97
Sixth Sunday after Epiphany	(The Ten Commandments 32)	Naaman the Leper 68	The Beatitudes: Jesus Talks about Blessings 98

The Common Lectionary continued

	Year A	Year B	Year C
Seventh Sunday after Epiphany	Jesus Talks about the Law of Israel *137*	A Man Who Could Not Walk *104*	Joseph Forgives His Brothers *18*
Eighth Sunday after Epiphany	Lilies of the Field *100* (Jesus Talks about the Law of Israel *137*)	(A Wedding at Cana *99*)	Can the Blind Lead the Blind? *110*
Last Sunday after Epiphany	The Transfiguration of Jesus *140*	Elijah at the Mountain of God *63* The Transfiguration of Jesus *140*	The Face of Moses Shines *36* The Transfiguration of Jesus *140*
First Sunday in Lent	The Garden of Eden *4* The Temptation of Jesus *95*	Noah and the Rainbow Covenant *5* The Temptation of Jesus *95*	The Temptation of Jesus *95*
Second Sunday in Lent	God Calls Abram *8* The Transfiguration of Jesus *140*	(Sarah and Abraham *10*) The Transfiguration of Jesus *140*	God's Covenant with Abram *9* The Transfiguration of Jesus *140*
Third Sunday in Lent	Water from the Rock *31*	The Ten Commandments *32* Jesus in the Temple *152*	Moses and the Burning Bush *23*
Fourth Sunday in Lent	The Anointing of David *52* The Man Who Was Born Blind *114*	The Babylonian Exile and Return *74*	(Joshua Crosses the Jordan *43*) The Prodigal Son *126*
Fifth Sunday in Lent	The Valley of Dry Bones *75* Jesus and His Friend Lazarus *141*	(The Valley of Dry Bones *75*)	(The Plagues and Passover *25*) (Crossing the Red Sea *27*)
Palm Sunday *Maundy Thursday* *Good Friday*	Jesus Rides into Jerusalem *151* Jesus in the Temple *152* The Last Supper *153* Jesus Washes His Disciples' Feet *154* Jesus Goes to the Cross *155*	Jesus Rides into Jerusalem *151* Jesus in the Temple *152* The Last Supper *153* Jesus Washes His Disciples' Feet *154* Jesus Goes to the Cross *155*	Jesus Rides into Jerusalem *151* Jesus in the Temple *152* The Last Supper *153* Jesus Washes His Disciples' Feet *154* Jesus Goes to the Cross *155*

The Common Lectionary continued

	Year A	Year B	Year C
Easter Vigil and Easter Day	God Makes the Universe *1* Crossing the Red Sea *27* (The Babylonian Exile and Return *74*) (The Valley of Dry Bones *75*) The First Easter *158*	God Makes the Universe *1* Crossing the Red Sea *27* (The Babylonian Exile and Return *74*) (The Valley of Dry Bones *75*) *The First Easter 158*	God Makes the Universe *1* Crossing the Red Sea *27* (The Babylonian Exile and Return *74*) (The Valley of Dry Bones *75*) The First Easter *158* The Lion and the Lamb *72*
Second Sunday of Easter	Thomas Sees the Risen Lord *161*	Thomas Sees the Risen Lord *161*	The Apostles in Jail *166* Thomas Sees the Risen Lord *161*
Third Sunday of Easter	The Road to Emmaus *161*	(The Man at the Beautiful Gate *165*)	Peter Goes Fishing *162* The Road to Damascus *168*
Fourth Sunday of Easter	The Good Shepherd *121*	The Good Shepherd *121*	(The Good Shepherd *121*) (Philip and the Man from Ethiopia *167*)
Fifth Sunday of Easter	(The Road to Damascus *168*)	Philip and the Man from Ethiopia *167*	Paul and Barnabas Are Called Gods *171* The Holy City *174*
Sixth Sunday of Easter	Paul Preaches in Athens *173*	Peter Baptizes a Roman *169*	The Holy City *174* (Paul Baptizes a Roman *169*)
Ascension Day and Seventh Sunday of Easter	Jesus Goes to His Father *163*	Jesus Goes to His Father *163*	Jesus Goes to His Father *163* An Earthquake at the Jail *172*
Pentecost	The Pentecost Story *164*	The Pentecost Story *164*	(The Tower of Babel *7*) The Pentecost Story *164*
Trinity Sunday	(Crossing the Red Sea *27*)	The Call of Isaiah *69*	(The Call of Isaiah *69*)
May 29–June 4	God's Covenant with Abram *9* A House Built on Rock *101*	The Anointing of David *52* Picking Grain on the Sabbath *105*	(Solomon Builds God's Temple *57*) The Centurion's Servant *111*
June 5–11	Jesus Asks Matthew to Follow Him *102*	(David and Goliath *54*)	(Elijah and the Widow's Bread *59*)

The Common Lectionary continued

	Year A	Year B	Year C
June 12–18	The Twelve Disciples 103 Jacob Becomes Israel 12	(Daniel in the Lions' Den 76) The Mustard Seed 106	A Woman Washes Jesus' Feet 150
June 19–25	(The Garden of Eden 4)	Jesus Calms the Storm 107	Peter Is Given His Name 129
June 26–July 2	(David and Goliath 54)	David Brings the Ark to Jerusalem 56 Jesus and the Little Girl 113	Elijah at the Mountain of God 63
July 3–9	The Birth of Moses 21	Jesus Teaches in the Synagogue 96	Jesus Sends Seventy-Two People to Teach 118
July 10–16	The Sower 116	The Twelve Disciples 96	Chariots of Fire 65 The Good Samaritan 119
July 17–23	The Wheat and the Weeds 117	Feeding Five Thousand People 112	Elisha Visits a Family 66 Mary and Martha 120
July 24–30	Moses and the Burning Bush 23	(Jesus Walks on Water 123)	Naaman the Leper 68 The Lord's Prayer 122
July 31–August 6	The Plagues and Passover 25 Feeding Five Thousand People 112	(Manna and Quails 29)	(Lilies of the Field 100)
August 7–13	Crossing the Red Sea 27 Jesus Walks on Water 123	(Spies in the Promised Land 41) (Lilies of the Field 100)	(Ten Women with Their Lamps 146)
August 14–20	Manna and Quails 29	(The Last Supper 153)	Jeremiah in the Well 73
August 21–27	Water from the Rock 31 Peter Is Given His Name 129	(Invitations to a Wedding 135)	(The Sheep and the Goats 149)
August 28–September 3	(The Widow's Penny 144)	(God's Law for Israel 37)	Invited to a Feast 124
September 4–10	(The Valley of Dry Bones 75)	The Desert Shall Bloom 70 Jesus Heals a Deaf Man 128	(Hannah and Samuel 49)

The Common Lectionary continued

	Year A	Year B	Year C
September 11–17	The Ten Commandments 32 The Wicked Servant 130	Peter Is Given His Name 129	(The Lost Sheep 125)
September 18–24	The Golden Calf 34 The Workers in the Vineyard 131	(The Pharisee and the Tax Collector 138)	(Joseph Becomes a Slave 14)
September 25–October 1	Two Sons 134	(The Man Who Was Born Blind 114)	(Joseph Forgives His Brothers 18)
October 2–8	(Joseph Becomes a Slave 14)	God Makes the First Man and Woman 3	(Daniel in the Lions' Den 76)
October 9–15	(Joseph and the Meaning of Dreams 16) Invitations to a Wedding 135	(The Birth of Moses 21)	Jesus Heals Ten Men 133
October 16–22	(Joseph Forgives His Brothers 18) (The Babylonian Exile and Return 74)	(Jesus Washes His Disciples' Feet 154)	The Poor Woman and the Judge 136
October 23–29	Jesus Talks about the Law of Israel 137 The Story of Ruth 48	The Blind Beggar 143	The Pharisee and the Tax Collector 138
October 30–November 5	(Jesus Washes His Disciples' Feet 154)	(The Good Samaritan 119) Jesus Talks about the Law of Israel 137	Zacchaeus in the Sycamore Tree 139
All Saints' Day	The Beatitudes: Jesus Talks about Blessings 98	The Holy City 174 Jesus and His Friend Lazarus 141	The Beatitudes: Jesus Talks about Blessings 98
November 6–12	Ten Women with Their Lamps 146	Elijah and the Widow's Bread 59 The Widow's Penny 144	(Moses and the Burning Bush 23)
November 13–19	A Story about Money 148	(Being Ready for God 145) (A Story about Money 144)	(The Tabernacle 39) (Solomon Builds God's Temple 57)